NOBODY
KNEW SHE
WAS THERE

ANDREW GLASCOE

NOBODY
KNEW SHE
WAS THERE

The True Story of a Mother Who Lost Her Way

authorHOUSE®

AuthorHouse™ LLC
1663 Liberty Drive
Bloomington, IN 47403
www.authorhouse.com
Phone: 1-800-839-8640

Published by AuthorHouse 06/06/2014

ISBN: 978-1-4918-5404-4 (sc)
ISBN: 978-1-4918-5403-7 (hc)
ISBN: 978-1-4918-5402-0 (e)

Library of Congress Control Number: 2014900912

To the family and friends who made this book possible

Contents

Chapter 1   Riverdale 1
Chapter 2   Whirlpool 4
Chapter 3   My Zen Monk 17
Chapter 4   Veils 20
Chapter 5   Mother's Day 41
Chapter 6   Not from Fine China 43
Chapter 7   The Madman 55
Chapter 8   Dinner at the Lido 57
Chapter 9   The Hoist 66
Chapter 10 Spiderweb 71
Chapter 11 Crowd of Pilgrims 85
Chapter 12 A House of Mirrors 93
Chapter 13 Red, Yellow, Blue, Green 107
Chapter 14 The Shield 112
Chapter 15 Slow-Motion Horror Film 128
Chapter 16 Spinning 133
Chapter 17 The Thread Finally Broken 145
Chapter 18 The Speedway 150
Chapter 19 Silence like a Shadow 160
Chapter 20 Beginnings and Endings 163
Chapter 21 Nobody Knew She Was There 168
Chapter 22 Spiral of Blood 172
Chapter 23 Dear Mother 177
Chapter 24 The Whole of Her Happiness 182

1

Riverdale

Iverdale—such an alluring name for what must once have been a lush valley, nestling a crystal-clear Don River as it meandered through Toronto on its way to Lake Ontario. Locating a hospital here for the treatment of tuberculosis seems so intuitively right: the oxygen from the profusion of trees and the tranquility of the original building's setting must have been life-giving to the hospital's first patients.

Now the Riverdale Hospital is a mockery of that memory. The crescent-shaped eight-storey affair, constructed in the 1960s, held some promise, at least on the outside, until some faceless bureaucrats decided to erect it behind the Don Jail. What could have been passing through the minds of those people, who must have known that the site had been a dumping ground for landfill, the scene of public hangings, and the location of the most notorious prison conditions in Canada? These gloomy associations hang over the Riverdale Hospital like a cloud of misery.

As I make my way down the hallway of this refuge for the elderly, the demented, and the dying, toward my mother's room, I feel I'm travelling through a tunnel where the strangest and most painful things happen. Sometimes I'm the detached observer, with my face pressed up against a windowpane in disbelief. At other times, I want to slow down to take it all in. A lot of the time, I can't get through fast enough. Most of the time, my heart goes out to those around me who are oblivious to the journey through their darkest days. Occasionally, I feel I can't take any more and have the urge to push an emergency button to bring it all to an absolute stop. Yet here I am, once again, deep inside the tunnel, looking for the light at the other end.

The hallway keeps curving like a swirling vortex. I peer into each room, a voyeur with a fascination for other people's suffering. In every room, another life is taking its course, winding down, eventually to be engulfed by unrelenting silence. I sometimes find myself a witness to vain efforts to speak, to utter a sound, to bellow, to scream, to bawl the eyes out—attempts to stave off the inevitable, to carve out some jewel against the background of noiselessness. Their result is a mad cacophony, as Wordsworth said, the sad, strange music of humanity.

I arrive at her room and cross the threshold to a marginally lighter discomfort. She resides in a large room with four beds. The outer wall is a curving window that brightens the room even on cloudy days. An old East Indian, Mr. Mohammed, sits by the bedside of his incapacitated wife. She stares blankly out the window. The patient next to her is asleep, while another bed across the room is empty. My mother lies in her bed by the window on the same side.

Today she is awake—barely. Her eyes are half open, and her grey hair is pulled up into a ponytail on the crown of her head. Her mouth, hanging open like a child's, reveals a few yellow teeth. Her legs are bent up to her waist; her arms are folded into her chest; and her hands are twisted into tight, clenched curls.

She grimaces when I press her knee, and her eyes register effrontery at having been touched by a proper stranger.

"Ma," I whisper in her good ear, "it's me. Your son—Andy."

I see no flinch of recognition. Even her acknowledgement of my presence lasts only as long as I stay within her line of vision.

An electronically regulated pump standing by her bedside measures out a milky grey substance in a suspended plastic bag and squeezes it through clear plastic tubes into her bloodstream. The stupid regularity of the IV machine, which I have named the Kangaroo after the manufacturer, measures the liquid's dosage in the exact amounts required to keep my mother here.

This is her only sustenance. She cannot feed herself, and she has not experienced the pleasure of tasting, eating, and swallowing for some three years.

She is unaware of this, as she is unaware of just about everything around her. This is an understatement. Hers is the face of oblivion—a face from which all semblance of mental activity has been removed. I don't know who she is anymore.

A tiny Zen monk, the chatterbox mystic who lives in the cave of my mind, suddenly appears to annoy me with his unflagging calmness and benevolence. Adorned in grey robes, he's as bald as a bowling ball, has only one eye, and walks with a limp. Uninvited, he frequently sticks his nose into my private life, trying to offer meaning where there is none.

"That's her original face," he says.

"Is that some kind of Zen joke?" I ask.

"You've heard the story of the original face, haven't you?"

"I think I'm about to hear it again."

"The Zen master gave a question to a monk searching for enlightenment: 'What's your original face?'"

"Meaning what?" I ask angrily.

"Obviously, he wasn't talking about his ordinary face but about his face before he was born."

"This is her face before she dies."

"Same thing."

"Is that supposed to enlighten me?"

My imaginary Zen monk never answers this question. He conveniently disappears when I ask it.

A tired but smiling nurse wheels the medication trolley into the room. Mr. Mohammed calls out to her.

"Is that for me?"

"Sure," she says playfully. "Do you think you need it?"

"You bet," he replies with a smile.

2

Whirlpool

By the time I realized that I hardly knew who my mother was, that I *needed* to unravel her deeply entangled story, there were few relatives I could turn to for help. My mother had lost most of her faculties, my father was dead, all my grandparents on both sides of the family were long gone, my aunt in Saskatchewan was ailing, one of my uncles had passed away, the other—still in Scotland—might as well be on another planet for all the interest we showed in each other, and my somewhat estranged brother was working in Houston. There were four grandchildren, only two of whom had any real contact with her. Other extended-family members, cousins of various ranks, had almost no connection to her and were dispersed, mostly to parts unknown. Besides, I had little or no relationship with most of them, and they would hardly welcome any attempt on my part to ask them for something like this. None of them had ever shown any great love for my mother anyway, and I had no reason to think this had changed, since neither she nor I had heard from them in all the years we had been in Canada.

As the son of Maggie and her husband, Bob Glascoe, who had died more than ten years earlier, I was afflicted with the compulsion to take stock, to settle the accounts before they were called in. It was as if this had become the great task of my life—to unravel the mysteries of my nuclear family, about which I knew so little.

My mother had been slowly and agonizingly crippled by Alzheimer's. It was as if she had stalled the car and was now unable to shift gears to drive home. She couldn't remember her name, and she had been rendered helpless and dependent on others for the essentials of her life. It was the appalling muteness of her condition that galled me. While the pain she endured in her last days was excruciatingly apparent in her facial expressions, she was singularly incapable of voicing that pain. She had lost almost all ability to communicate. I couldn't ask her what help she needed, let alone any of the questions I had long wanted to put to her. She had lost not only the capacity to articulate her own experience but also the power to recognize that a question was being asked of her in the first place.

I tried to remember what she had been like. Groping in the darkness of recollected territory, I felt like a child abandoned by the roadside. My mother was a long way off in the distance; I was no longer sure I could make out any of her features. I wasn't even sure she was there anymore. Sometimes I thought I heard her calling my name. Here I was, in my fifties, still a barefoot child tramping in the direction of my mother's voice.

And which direction was the voice coming from? What could I remember of the past? How much had I forgotten? What had I never known in the first place? Was it a remembrance of things past or an anticipation of what was to come, since my mother had still to unfold for me? Nothing seemed clear, except that I was caught in a whirlpool that was gradually engulfing me—us, my entire family. I had to find my mother before it was too late, before I drowned in the waters of my own procrastination.

I decided to follow the blood connection in her grandchildren first, with my brother's son and my own daughter. They would carry memories of my mother into the future, and perhaps they knew something I didn't. I started with my nephew, young Bobbie, who had been named after my older brother, Robert, who in turn was named after my father, Bob Glascoe.

Bobbie was born a day later than my daughter—Anastasia, or Ana—which deprived his mother of the credit for producing the first grandchild in the family. This was of no consequence to Bobbie; he loved his cousin to death and never tired of showing it, even though she didn't always reciprocate. Not long after Bobbie was born, my brother and his wife, Elaine, decided they were leaving Canada to return to her former homeland, England. My brother told me they were doing this "so we could have some trees around us." Leaving Canada, home of some of the great forests of the world, to find trees in England? Either Robert was doing a bad job of being circumspect or he was so naive that it amounted to remarkable ignorance. I preferred to believe the former. He was, in fact, running away from his parents—for the second time in his life— but ended up returning to Canada a couple years later to settle at some distance from them in Ottawa. The result was that his son, Bobbie, was about five years old before he got to know his grandparents on this side of the Atlantic.

He talked of meeting them first in Glasgow on one of their visits "back home" and then again as he crossed the ocean of his childhood memory in Toronto. As he spoke, the family whirlpool began to spin.

"When we were back in Canada, I stayed with them in Toronto for a few days," he recalled. "I remember Circe, the cat, keeping me awake at night. After that, I used to visit in the summer, at the Lido, on Lakeshore Road. I'd come for a month. Mom and Dad seemed to need to get rid of me for a while once a year."

My mother and father, Maggie and Bob, had a knack for selective living of the worst kind—choosing to live in the most miserable apartment buildings around. The Lido was one of those 1950s jobs, a drab little three-storey dirty-red brick box in a perpetual state of disrepair. The hallways smelled because they weren't ventilated properly, and the dim lighting only added to the already-dreary atmosphere. The apartments were small, dark, and moldy. If anything in the building worked, it worked badly. The landlords should have been charged with a crime for renting out a dump like that. My parents never seemed to mind, though, and accepted it. They were both working in low-paying jobs and couldn't afford high rents, and they seemed to seek out places like that as a kind of self-inflicted punishment for some undefined infraction.

"The most vivid memories I have of Nana and Granpa," Bobbie said, "were when Ana was there. I remember you poring over books!" He laughed. "That made me think I never wanted to go to university."

"I was doing graduate work then," I explained. "I wasn't living there, but I came over a few times and took you and Ana to the local pool. I remember throwing the two of you around in the shallow end. You used to love that. I'd lift you up and just toss you back in with a huge splash. You were a little harder to lift than Ana, as I recall."

I had always been slim, but at that time, I was strong enough from doing martial arts to enjoy horsing around with this youngster—the same youngster who had grown to dwarf me in my middle age and make me feel like a scarecrow with clothes dangling from my frame. He had always been a tall, big-boned boy; now, in his early thirties, he was six foot four and showing evidence of an expanding waistline. Endowed with the flat Glascoe feet, he moved slowly like a giant, friendly animal with the gentle soul of a lamb, a quick wit, and a sharp intelligence.

"You took us over to Maria's mom's place one time for spaghetti," he recalled with a gleeful, childlike smile.

"Maria and I were divorced by then," I said. "But I still saw her and her family in those days. Her dad, Leonardo, made the best spaghetti around. It was a Sunday afternoon ritual for years."

"There was some sort of Italian festival going on in the park by their house."

"Yes," I said, "they lived in Mimico. It was a mostly Italian neighborhood then."

"They had races, games, and food. I was big for my age. I won three or four of the races."

"We had some pizza there after the races," I reminded him. "That's when I got my first taste of food poisoning. I was violently ill. I was living with my girlfriend, Adèle, by then, and I tried to get home on the bus. But I had to call my parents from the subway to come and get me. I just couldn't make it. And at their house, I was bringing up every hour. I even started to hallucinate! Mom was afraid I was going to die. Aunt Betty and Cousin Eileen, who were visiting from Saskatchewan, were trying to reassure Mom, who was hyper-anxious. Eileen—she was about sixteen at the time—peeked at me occasionally from the living room. I was in the bedroom, but she was afraid to come near me in case she caught something."

"Ana and I kept track of how many times you threw up," Bobbie said with a giggle. "Twenty-eight times!"

"I seem to remember hearing you two frolicking around, completely oblivious to my predicament."

"We drove Nana nuts. There was a convenience store across the street that used to sell a lot of junk. But it was cheap, so we used to buy stuff there for fun. We bought some fake puke once and laid it across the side of the bathtub. I called Nana and said, 'I've just been sick!' She freaked out and tried to wipe it up. When she discovered it was fake, boy, was she mad."

"Mom told me," I said, "that each of you alone was fine but that the two of you together turned into 'wee devils. I'm no' goannie invite them here again at the same time,' she'd say!"

"She used to make that Ayrshire bacon, flat pork sausage, and toasted Scotch 'breed,' as she called it. You could never get that stuff anywhere else. It was a real treat."

"The typical greasy Scotch breakfast," I moaned.

Bobbie talked happily of the many summer visits to my parents' place, of coming to my house once, and of a trip to Betty's farm. Despite the fracture between his parents and mine, he had repeatedly ventured across the abyss to keep in touch with both his grandparents, his cousin, and me.

"Generally, Granpa wasn't around that much," he recalled. "He was working the night shift. When he was at home, there wasn't much conversation. I didn't really warm up to him until I was older. Nana always seemed a bit batty, running around in a frenzy most of the time. Circe was the first cat I'd ever seen that would hiss and growl anytime you came near her. She used to hide under the bed or the chairs, but one time, Nana dragged her out—she was the only one who could touch that cat—and while she was holding Circe in her arms, the cat peed all across the floor. I'll never forget that. It was a truly psychotic cat."

"Your nana was totally dependent on the cat," I said in the way of a feeble explanation. "Circe was a house cat who literally never went outside in the open air. The only model for that cat's behavior was your nana. Circe's anxiety was a mirror image of hers. The two of them spent so much time together—at night, when your granpa was on night shift, and during the day, when he was mostly asleep. By this time, my mom and dad had no friends. They lived in a state of restrained frenzy."

"For years, even up until I was in my late teens," Bobbie said, "I would come and stay with them for a month. There wasn't much for me to do, but I was glad for the opportunity to be here in Toronto."

"Ana wasn't around?"

"No, she had her own friends by then."

Bobbie made a good show of hiding his feelings on this, but obviously, it had been a real disappointment to him. He seemed to be half in love with his cousin, but for some reason, Ana seemed rather cooler toward him. I never understood why.

"I used to get on the subway and ride downtown," he said. "Walk around, shop, go to movies. Staying inside was just not an option. Their apartment was a small one-bedroom, not really big enough to have a teenager there for weeks on end. Granpa was always a drinker, and Nana would ration it out. She spent a lot of time hiding the booze. So much of the fuss between them was about that."

"It must have been an unhappy time for you there."

"No," he replied firmly. "It didn't bother me. They insisted on sleeping in the living room, so I had the bedroom. But the place had no air-conditioning. Nana would keep the windows shut so Circe couldn't escape. The apartment was a heat trap."

This was how my parents had lived their broken lives—with all the doors and windows closed. Coming too late to Canada, having too few of the social graces and far too many serious needs that could never be met, they were afraid to venture into the larger community. Or if they did, they made short work of the attempt. In the end, they retreated to their hovel and locked themselves in, finally, with the cat substituting for the children who had flown the coop. All three of them craved an escape, but neither my mother nor my father knew how to make it happen.

Bobbie spoke again. "One time, when I was about fifteen years old, I guess, Granpa told me all about the war. That's when I realized that Burma was Vietnam ten times over. I don't think the Burma guys got the recognition those Vietnam guys got. That was an eye-opener for me. It explained a lot about Granpa."

Robert, it seems, had never talked to his son about any of this stuff. In fact, my brother hardly ever spoke about his parents to his children. Bobbie was the only one of three boys who, on his own and consistently, tried to reach out to his clearly struggling grandparents. But his memories were fragmented and disorganized like an unfinished jigsaw puzzle, and Bobbie shifted from one thing to another like a kid looking to discern a pattern in the chaos of ill-defined pieces.

"I remember Granpa's car, that old yellow Maverick. What a clunker! Things were falling off it all the time. The door handles were literally glued on. I once asked him and Nana to drive me to the Cineplex downtown. Crazy thing to do, but I didn't realize until then how stressed out he was about driving."

"He learned to drive only when he came to Canada," I replied. "When he was in his late forties. It was then I began to understand just how deeply his war experiences had scarred him. Anything new he had to learn—whatever required all his resources and attention—he had serious trouble coping with."

"Just driving to the shopping mall was tough," said Bobbie. "Granpa was perpetually grumpy, and Nan nagged him about which way to turn. They got lost going to the Cineplex, and I couldn't help them, because I didn't know Toronto."

"When I first moved in with Adèle," I said, Bobbie's recollections prompting mine, "we lived in an apartment above the shopping mall at Yonge and Eglinton. My parents came to visit and parked in the underground lot downstairs. When they left, I went down with them, got into the car, and helped them navigate their way onto the street. I pointed them in the direction to get out of the city centre. Back upstairs, I went out onto the balcony with Adèle for a breather—having them over was a serious strain for us! From there, Adèle and I stood and laughed as we watched them driving around the block for a second and third time because they couldn't follow the directions I gave them. Doing two stressful things at once was impossible for Dad. He could drive but not navigate. Mom was the navigator but with no sense of direction. In the midst of this, they'd be fighting like tomcats about who was to blame for it all."

This car scene was one of many screwy little dramas that just kept happening throughout my parents' lives. They were, by this time, in their early sixties. She was pale, thin, and hyperactive from years of poor nourishment, heavy smoking, and too much coffee. He was a mostly bald man with a slim build, but he was hard and strong from working as a shipper, loading tractor trailers for a living. Together, they were a tragicomic, slapstick duo in an absurd drama that kept repeating itself. Each drove the other crazy while they both waited, it seemed, for the Godot who never came.

"Talking about blame," young Bobbie said in a darker tone, "my mom never liked yours."

I hadn't expected him to take the initiative in mentioning this thorny relationship and had been wondering how I would raise the issue. But Bobbie had seen the opening and hadn't hesitated.

"It had nothing to do with me," he hastily pointed out. "Nana was nice to me, and she was my grandmother. So I had a problem with Mom's problem. Once, Mom was trashing Nana for something long forgotten. I said to her, 'Why do you always talk that way about Nana?' I wished that she wouldn't say anything to me about it. She always had very specific beefs which, even at that time, went way back before I was born to when she and Dad were first married. That was twenty years earlier, and now it's thirty-five years on and still not forgotten. I could never understand that. I still don't. The things Mom said were always hard for me to hear. To say them to a kid just wasn't right. You could say to an adult, 'Look, I can't stand your grandmother,' and then talk about it. But to say this to me as a kid was confusing and hurtful. I knew Nana was a bit crazy, sure, but she wasn't evil. And she wouldn't have done something evil to anyone, let alone me."

I was astonished. Through all the years of this feud between my mother and Elaine, I had never once heard anything from my brother that came close to acknowledging the problem, let alone recognizing Elaine's role in it. His signature response was to ignore it, to do absolutely nothing. I thought it was heroic that young Bobbie had survived all those efforts by his mom to trash his grandmother, in the face of his father's passivity, and that in the meantime, he had developed such a sane perspective on it.

Bobbie said, "I remember only one happy visit my grandparents made to our house. They brought over a kilt—I guess it was your old kilt."

"Yes, they dressed me up for the '51 London Exhibition."

"My younger brother, Johnny, tried it on, and it fit. He was about the same age as you were then. Johnny did a little jig, and that made Granpa laugh. I'll never forget that; he didn't laugh that often. It was hard to get a chuckle out of him at the best of times. He was always grumpy, and that's why Mom couldn't stand him. He just never seemed to be happy. I don't know what it is about Scots. It seems so typical. The notorious Scottish dourness?"

"Yeah," I replied, but rather feebly because I knew that there was nothing typical about my father's condition.

Bob Glascoe, a seriously depressed man, had been deeply damaged by the war. There were no options for people like him after the war— there was no psychotherapy for the war-torn soldiers who had thought peacetime was going to be easy. Bob was one of perhaps millions who, after surviving such a war, had learned to function in ordinary life while enduring the worst kinds of personality disorders. That Bob functioned badly was no surprise; the surprise was that he could function at all.

"I remember Granpa dying," young Bobbie said.

"How did you find out?"

"Dad told me. It was right at the end of the school year. That's why I didn't go to the funeral. I could've gotten out of exams, but I was avoiding it. I had never been to a funeral, and I didn't want this to be my first. I was shocked when he died. I couldn't figure out why he took his own life."

I was surprised to hear Bobbie bring up this "unmentionable" issue. I had always been fond of the boy; now I admired him.

"Your grandfather had been through hell a long time before this," I said.

"I guess he was really sick. I never really understood what happened there. I never got the story."

"He had an operation for some sort of blood-clot problem," I told him. "But that was successfully resolved. He was later troubled by his prostate and thought he might have cancer. After he died, an autopsy was performed on him—they do that in suicide cases—and they didn't find any cancer."

"That's not the end of the story, though, is it?" he said.

"Amazingly, when I think of it now, my mom and dad were in good physical shape for people who never really took care of themselves or had regular checkups—maybe *because* they rarely went to doctors. She was thin but strong boned, and she moved with the energy of a squirrel, in fits and starts. After years of working as a packer on the loading docks of big tractor trailers, he had the physique of a young man—muscular arms and a strong upper body. But the war destroyed his nerves and his ability to cope with the stress of living. So doing simple day-to-day tasks like driving to the shopping mall were painful for him.

"Then there was my mom's gradually declining mental capacity. When you talked to her on the phone, as your dad did occasionally, she seemed fine—which explains why he never understood until long afterward what condition she was in. But when you lived with her every day, as poor old Bob did, it was a very different story. She was forgetting things, unable to follow instructions, inventing stories about mistresses he never had, and accusing him of taking her 'best glasses' to 'that woman's' apartment; into the bargain, she was unable look after him or the house way she used to.

"He was on the receiving end of this for a long time before I was able to see what was happening. And I, who was the closest person to them, didn't realize the pressure he was under until after he died, when I became her chief caregiver and the target of her anxieties. I had to run over to her apartment every day to make sure she ate, bathed, and went to bed without wandering away or burning the house down.

"Dad had been shattered by the war, had worked himself to the bone in the most menial and miserable jobs around, and then, just when he retired, discovered that his wife was going batty and that no one else seemed to see it, let alone offer help. He was at his wits' end about what to do. He had no idea how to talk about it to anyone, not even to me.

"I was away in Europe when the crisis began to peak. I got letters from both Mom and Dad. His letters always said the same thing, except his handwriting deteriorated each time until it was little more than a scrawl. I knew something was seriously wrong, but I didn't know what it was. I always thought that Mom was peculiar—she had been a source of embarrassment to me since my teenage years. I couldn't see much that was different in her now, especially from three thousand miles away.

"When I got back in April of '84, I realized that Dad had anxiously been waiting for me to come back. I was immediately on the phone with them and over at their house several times a week. Meanwhile, I was very sick myself—sicker than I had ever been in my life—and struggling just to stay functional. Adèle was hospitalized for an emergency operation on misdiagnosed gallstones, and Ana—she was fifteen then—had dropped out of school.

"All of this going on at the same time prevented me from seeing what came next. Dad's first suicide attempt. I remember how the news came. Adèle picked up the call. 'Your dad's just taken an overdose! They've rushed him to East General Hospital." I got there shortly after they pumped his stomach. He was really shaken up and looked none too happy about surviving.

"I made an appointment with the psychiatrist at East General for the next day. I picked up both Mom and Dad and took them there myself. While we were sitting in the cafeteria, waiting for our appointment, Mom toddled off to the bathroom. She ended up inadvertently locking herself in the stall, went into a panic, and called for help, but nobody heard her. Eventually, she climbed over the door of the stall and escaped.

"All of this gave me time for a quick shakedown talk with Dad. But as you know, he wasn't a man of many words. He had a hell of a time telling me what the trouble was. 'Your mither's saying things she shouldnae be saying.' He couldn't bring himself to say that she was going out of her mind, but that's what he thought. One of the symptoms in her case was the development of a ferocious paranoia. 'She's accusin' me of doin' things I never did.' He was hurting badly, and he was embarrassed.

"I saw Mom coming back, so I told him we would talk some more on Wednesday, only two days away, when I was scheduled to take him to an appointment with a urologist. On Wednesday, Mom phoned me. She was screaming hysterically into the phone. 'He's done it again! He's done it again!' Then another voice, a man's, was on the phone: 'Hello, sir. I'm a fireman. I think you should come here as quickly as possible. Your dad has been in an accident.' I broke the speed limit many times over getting to their place that morning, but the deed was already done."

"A really screwed-up couple," Bobbie mused. "But when they're your grandparents, you don't think of it that way."

"Granpa had lost the will to live a long time before," I told him. "If there was one thing that destroyed him, it was guilt."

"About what?"

"Surviving the war. He survived a skirmish in which his best friend was shot through the neck by a sniper in the Burmese jungle. He told me, 'I'll never forget the squeal he let out as he fell beside me.' And he didn't. He was still telling me that story forty years later. He also survived the long march out of the jungle, breaking through Japanese lines, to escape after their mission was over. Most of the men in his battalion were killed by snipers or shot in firefights with the Japanese troops; others succumbed to yellow fever, dengue, or any number of other diseases on the long march home. I saw my dad bedridden with what he called 'the shakes,' malaria, more than once long after the war was over."

"Amazing that someone can carry guilt like that for so long," Bobbie said. "Now I understand why he always had to have a drink when he was speaking about the war."

We sat silently for several minutes, thinking about all that had happened.

"After Granpa died, things were different," Bobbie went on with a heavier tone in his voice. "I was in second year at university when I phoned Nana. 'A couple of my friends and I are coming to Toronto tomorrow,' I said to her. 'Can we stay the night?' I knew it was a squeeze, but we were poor students.

"Anyway, she was happy about it and said yes right off. But when we arrived, she was nowhere to be found. We waited around for a long time and then went off to get something to eat. When we came back, she was home and thrilled but totally surprised to see us. That was when she was forgetting everything."

My mother had been showing symptoms of Alzheimer's for years, although it was only in hindsight that I realized this. By this time, when she was in her mid-sixties, she was forgetting things five minutes after saying them, could not take instructions, and was barely able to look after herself. I had taken her to the specialists at Toronto General and was going over to see her more or less daily while I waited for the assessments. She was in a desperate state. So was I.

"She kept asking us if we were hungry," Bobbie remembered. "'No, we're fine,' I'd say. I knew she was off by then. She could still do everything, but she had no short-term memory. She was forgetting her way around. This visit was a shocker."

"I was most worried about her burning down the apartment," I said. "Leaving something on the stove when she went out."

"When I look back on all this now, though," Bobbie said, "I still have good memories about them. Ana and I had great laughs with Nana. We'd take advantage of her battiness, but she always took good care of us. She overfed us and never held us back from doing what we wanted to do. Granpa too—he'd drive us wherever we wanted to go, no matter how much stress it caused him."

"They were essentially good, decent people," I hastily added. "They loved you kids. The war experience seems to have been the mother of all their traumas."

"We lucked out," Bobby said. "We haven't had any traumas like that so far."

I wasn't sure whom he was referring to as "we," and I didn't want to say anything about the hubris of such a remark. Bobbie would have to find out what this meant in the only way that convinces any of us: when we too are drawn into the whirlpool of suffering.

3

My Zen Monk

I take the elevator as usual to the eighth floor and step into the crescent-moon-shaped hallway. The walls are psychedelic pink; the floor tiles are the usual bland beige. The pong in the air today is far worse than usual. Maybe it's the time of day. Sometimes the stench stays in my nostrils long after I leave—a combination of food, medication, shit, urine, and vomit.

Just as I think I'm going to be sick, an old lady shuffling in the middle of the hallway ahead of me stops. She looks down with intense curiosity at the mess she's made at her feet. I pass by quickly and, without pausing at the nursing station, alert the staff.

"Somebody's lost the contents of her bowels in the hallway."

"Shit!" cries the nurse, quite unaware of the irony.

I dive into my mother's room and take a deep breath of the fresh air coming in through the open windows. I lean over to give Mom a kiss on the forehead. She is startled by my touch. Her eyes stare uncomprehendingly. Her mouth hangs open, and her tongue droops over her bottom teeth and lips.

A nurse, wheeling her medication trolley past us, turns away when she sees me leaning over my mother, stroking her head.

"I'll come back later," she says with an awkward smile.

"Is that for me?" Mr. Mohammed asks, as he always does. He is engaged in his daily ritual of sitting with his bedridden wife.

"One of these days, Mr. Mohammed," the nurse says with a laugh, "I'm going to give you some."

She leaves the room and passes out of sight momentarily. Then, in an afterthought, she pops her head back in the door.

"Looking for a chair?" she asks me.

"Yes, please."

"There's one out here."

For the first time since I've been visiting my mother at Riverdale, which is more than two years now, someone has offered me a chair. I sit down between the window and her bedside because my mother is facing in this direction. I turn my eyes to the outside world, the Don Valley Parkway below. The cars roar by. In the playing field on the other side of the freeway, a group of kids like those dwarfish figures in a Breughel landscape seems to perform odd rituals, congregating and alternately dispersing around something too small to see from this distance. The trees on the valley slopes, not having recovered yet from the assault of winter, stand like rigid, weary ghosts under the cold glare of the sun. In the background are the steel, concrete, and glass boxes of the city.

"What a view you have, Ma," I whisper to her. "You can survey the craziness from the safety of your little cell."

Another nurse comes in with a couple of cans of feed for the IV feeder—the Kangaroo—that substitutes for my mother's own now-useless apparatus. The nurse looks at me with mild irritation, as if I'm an obstacle to her routine.

"Do you need to get in here?" I ask, getting up from my seat. "Or would you like me to poke you in the eye?" I whisper unkindly under my breath.

"Yes," she says impatiently. "I need to give her some medicine."

She fills up the clear plastic bag with the grey liquid and re-programs the Kangaroo. The commotion has drawn the attention of my mother. As if she has forgotten how to move her head, she rolls her eyes, trying to catch sight of whatever is making the noise. When the nurse leaves, Mother retreats to her semiconscious state, staring blankly through the window at the blue sky.

I sit down again, shaking my head.

"What sort of life is going on here?" I whisper to myself.

This is the kind of signal my Zen monk often responds to. I can rely on him to pop up like burned bread from a toaster, as always the image of an impossibly pure compassion.

"It's not living," I say to him as he leans over my chair from behind.

"No?"

"Just the opposite."

My monk is not impressed.

"Death," I continue, "not life, is taking its course. Stupidly, dumbly, obtusely, we've slowed the process down, boxed it in. But all the pus is oozing out, and all its odors and noises fill the air. Death is imprisoned in a make-work project for the living. There's nothing to be done."

Sitting down on the bed, the monk leans over and touches my mother's leg. He turns to me and smiles benevolently.

"Help me!" I whisper.

"I *am* helping you," he says, smiling.

"Don't give me that silent-smile treatment!"

"You seem to have all the answers. There's nothing to be done—didn't you say that?"

"Damn you!" I say in an angry whisper so as not to attract the attention of Mr. Mohammed across the room.

"Thanks for those words," the Zen monk says. He is unperturbed. "Someday I'll give them back to you."

He sees the anger rising in my face again. He gets up from the bed and stands by the window as if preparing to make a quick exit.

"You've got an answer for everything but that anger of yours," he lectures. "Why? What is it you're so angry about?"

Unable to contain my mood, I jump up from my chair to grab him by his ears. But he vanishes before I touch him.

Mr. Mohammed turns and smiles in my direction. I nod as I pick up my bag to leave.

4
Veils

It was a bit odd to think that in order to know my mother, I had to ask for my daughter's help. While my mother had become a mostly mute, disturbed creature, Ana had developed into an articulate thirty-year-old with sharp powers of observation and a strong sense of family justice. At the age of nine, as a child of divorced parents, she had come to live with me. It was a turn of events that was agreeable to everyone at the time—Ana; my former wife, Maria; and me. This was not the result of painful legal wrangling but a happy arrangement reached by mutual goodwill and careful negotiations. When we later moved in with the woman I subsequently married, Adèle, Ana came to relish the fact that she had two mothers—her biological mom and her stepmom.

But the trauma of the divorce eventually began to surface. Ana was deeply anxious about love and stability. By the time she turned sixteen, she had a captivatingly attractive face. She and I disagreed over curfews, and she became furiously defiant. Eventually, she became pregnant. When I forced her to give up the baby for adoption, Ana was deeply resentful. Knowing how much I wanted her to have an education, she dropped out of school, and in an act of spite against my left-wing leanings, she found a job in the financial industry. She went to live with a boyfriend whom she eventually married and then divorced a few years later. By the time she was thirty, Ana had gone through more emotional upheavals than many people do in a lifetime. But somehow the bond between us remained strong.

"I couldn't go to see her," Ana told me when I asked why she so rarely visited her grandmother in the chronic care hospital. "I can't stand places like that. They're so depressing."

"They're part of life."

"Yeah, but all those old people packed together." She grimaced. "Like wrecked cars in a dump."

She had a point. The institutionalized isolation of old age turned me off too. But I needed to rationalize. "You shouldn't shrink from it. You need to face up to things like that. No matter how unpleasant."

"I suppose. But there's more to it than that."

"Such as?"

"I never really forgave her."

"For what?"

"For what she did to Papa."

Papa was the name she used for my father; she used *Nana* for my mother. The maternal grandparents became *Granma* and *Granpa*. I don't know who invented those names, but it seemed an eminently sensible way to help a child to distinguish one set of grandparents from the other. The variability of names we used in our family, which wasn't unlike others in this regard, would become significant for me later, however, particularly in the case of my mother.

"What do you mean?" I asked.

I'd once had misgivings about my mother's treatment of my father in his last years too, but I wanted to hear Ana's story on this. I was beginning to feel that I might have to defend my mother against the charges I anticipated coming from my daughter. The one was no saint, to be sure, but the other bore grudges too easily—particularly, I had noticed, against other women. This was a characteristic that, ironically, was all too apparent in my mother. It was not the first time I had noticed my mother's habits and attitudes re-emerging in the rest of us.

"I adored her, you know. But I was wary of her," Ana said.

"Why?"

"Nana hid things from you. Her nasty—very nasty—side. The side she was so quick to display to everybody else. Like the way she treated my other grandparents."

Andrew Glascoe

The other grandparents were my former in-laws, Leonardo and Kate. He was an Italian immigrant who all his life had worked on the railroad. She was a divorcée from Mimico who had lived for a while in Northern Ontario and who had two children from an earlier marriage. He was a quiet, gentle Italian immigrant whom most people, particularly his wife, ignored. She was a tiny, hard-headed woman with a fiery temper. For reasons that were never clear to anyone, he lived most of his married life in separate quarters in the basement of a bungalow in Etobicoke, while she ruled the roost up above. Both doted over their granddaughter.

"I used to love going over to their house. Even though I sensed some problem between them, I mainly had a good time. Nobody but me used to pay attention to Grandpa, so he played with me and let me help him in the garden. He was gentle and tender with me—and so docile in front of everyone else. But he used to get mad when Nana came around." Ana took a breath. "He had no time for her. He'd swear under his breath when he opened the door.

"Nana was a real tension creator, and she was rarely challenged by anyone. But amazingly, Grandpa sometimes took her on. She used to launch into diatribes against people she didn't like. Once it was the pope, who she hated. Grandpa responded by attacking the queen. 'The Catholics want to control the world,' she said, oblivious to the fact that Grandpa was a Catholic, 'but they won't control me.' Grandpa answered by saying, 'The queen steals from the poor. She's just a big robber!' The two of them scrapped while Grandma tried to change the subject, and everyone else just snickered."

"Sounds eminently stupid."

"It was, I guess. Except that to me, as a child, it was upsetting."

I had often admired my daughter's youthful beauty, but now while she talked, I could see the lines beginning to form under the eyes—lines not so much of age as of experience, of distress and anxiety.

"The worst scenario I remember, though, happened when you and Mom went somewhere on holiday without me. I was like a rag doll that each set of grandparents had been given equal time to play with. I don't recall the details—I must have been, what age?"

"Four or five. I can't remember exactly."

"I didn't want to leave Grandma's house. But Nana insisted. In fact, this is the only time I remember her clashing with Grandma. 'She doesn't want to go, for Chrissakes!' Grandma said. 'Leave her for another day.' But Nana would have none of it. 'Your daddy'll be angry if you don't come with me,' she said. She picked me up kicking and screaming to carry me off to the car. I remember how both Papa and Grandpa kept their distance from all this. One was sitting in the car, shaking his head, and the other was standing in a corner of the living room, muttering to himself."

Ana paused and looked at me, as she had many times during this conversation, scrutinizing my face for my reaction before she continued.

"Mom was afraid of her, you know."

"Maria? Afraid of Nana? Really?"

Ana nodded. "The things Nana would say to her when you weren't there—or when you were out of earshot. Remember those Sunday visits that would go on forever? Well, she would sit there with a smile on her face, talking to Mom until you left the room, and then she would say something outlandish like 'You don't deserve someone like him.' Right out of the blue. In response to nothing."

"Why didn't your mom tell me this?"

"Because you wouldn't believe her," she said, looking me in the eye.

I was embarrassed that my attachment to my mother had left me so blind and uncritical of her. Mom had never tired of doing things for me—making dinners, sewing, washing dishes. Had I really been so easily deceived? I averted my eyes from Ana's.

"Mom never said anything in reply to these statements," Ana said. "She was afraid of Nana's power over you. She always backed away. Later on, after you and Mom split up, Nana used to say to me, 'I love your mom.' I knew, even then as a child, that this was bullshit. I thought she was a bit odd, but as a little girl, I couldn't really figure it all out. When I look back now, I often wonder if she was schizoid."

Whatever pain Ana had felt as a result of all this was long gone. She was curiously cool in conducting this analysis of her grandmother's psyche. But this time, my mother had turned sixty and dyed her hair almost blonde. She was an anxiety-driven woman who made others nervous just watching her.

"She was so hostile to both her daughters-in-law," said Ana. "But Elaine wasn't a pushover like Mom."

When he was eighteen, my brother Robert left Scotland to come to Canada alone. After arriving, he met and married another ex-Brit, Elaine, before his parents and I joined him here. He was a tall, handsome guy, and she was a busty blonde who liked to laugh. But Elaine was a London cockney with a strange ingrained cultural snobbery. If you listened to what she said, you had to conclude that she had come to Canada because everything in England was better!

Elaine was deeply ambivalent toward my daughter. On the one hand, Elaine dearly wanted to take her niece, Ana, under her wing because she longed for a daughter. On the other hand, because Ana had been born a day before her own son, Bobbie, Elaine had been robbed of the opportunity to produce the first grandchild in the family. Her relationship with her mother-in-law, while it lasted, was acrimonious. This, however, was not her fault alone or even primarily, as Ana soon made vividly clear.

"One time, I went with them to visit Uncle Robert and Aunt Elaine, who'd just finished building the little guesthouse on their property. Nana trashed Elaine all the way from Toronto to Ottawa. By the time we got there, I had knots in my stomach. But Aunt Elaine welcomed us with the usual smiles, hugs, and kisses. Everything seemed hunky-dory. We had our own place in the guesthouse, and there was lots of room for everybody. But next morning, Nana wanted to leave. She had decided that Aunt Elaine had put us in the cottage because she didn't want us in the main house. She was furious that we didn't have a kettle to make tea, though Elaine had told us to come inside for breakfast. But Nana insisted we weren't going to stay without a kettle. And she began to pack up. But Papa said, 'I'm not going anywhere.' Nana was furious. 'That bitch!' she said. 'You think I'm going to let her get away with this?' Papa—this was one of the few times I saw him stand up to her—ordered her to sit tight and get used to it."

"So what happened after that?"

"Nana said nothing when Uncle Robert was around, but she had a miserable time. You could tell she was fuming inside. I managed to escape most of the time by playing outside with Cousin Bobbie. I remember seeing one scuffle between Nana and Aunt Elaine when we were in the kitchen alone, making breakfast on the Sunday morning before we left. Elaine asked us if we were comfortable in the guesthouse. 'What do you care if we weren't?' Nana said. 'This is the last time I'm coming here, you bitch.' Well, Aunt Elaine stopped what she was doing and turned to Nana. 'That's one time too many for me.'"

"I'll bet the two of them smiled all the way through breakfast anyway."

"Yeah, but there were no hugs and kisses when we left."

Ana continued watching me to see if any of this upset or disturbed me. It did. The veils were beginning to lift from my illusions about my mother.

She went on. "Cousin Bobbie and I stayed with her for a couple of weeks one summer when we were about eleven. She was a lot of fun in those days. It was easy to take the mickey out of her, and when she lost her temper, it wasn't serious. We played practical jokes on her, and we could see her trying to keep from laughing when she scolded us and promised to tell our daddies—which we knew she wouldn't do. She was very protective that way. I remember her telling you that I was a 'wee doll.'"

Ana said this with the mischievous giggle of the little girl she sometimes became during this conversation, looking at her daddy with a childlike glance as if to avoid a scolding.

"One time," she continued, "we sneaked flavored candy crystals into bed with us. As soon as Nana left us alone, we started eating them. They were all over the bed." Ana cackled. "We woke up in the middle of the night all sticky, and we were giggling and snickering. This roused her, and she gave us hell. The sheets were stained with yellow and purple food dye. She bitched at us constantly while changing the bedding and eventually became exasperated with the two of us always freaking her out. In the end, we wore her down, I guess. We never got invited together again. Did she ever say anything to you about this?"

"Just that you were a 'pair o' wee bisms.'"

"Wee bisms?"

"Scotch for 'little devils.'"

"When I went to stay with her on my own, things were different. Papa worked nights and wouldn't arrive home until midnight. She would send me to bed at my regular time and wake me up an hour before he came home. She would grill sausages and roast cheese over Scotch bread for his meal. When she saw him coming down the driveway of the apartment building, she'd cry out, 'There he is! Quick—let's go.' Then she would send me down the hall to welcome him home. I'd call out to him as he came in the back door and run to meet him. He loved it when I ran to meet him. He would smile in that sad way of his, reach out to pull my one hand into his, and give me his lunch box to carry in the other. I remember that three fingers were missing from his right hand."

Ana never disguised her partiality for her papa. When she talked about him, her voice changed, becoming softer, gentler. Tears sometimes welled up in her eyes. Although my old man had the physique of a younger man, he was worn out by the arduous work and long night-shift hours for years at a time. What was left of his hair was still jet black, and you could see the features of the once-handsome soldier. His arms were decorated with tattoos from the war days.

"It was strange, though," Ana continued. "Nana would encourage me to be close to Papa, but then we were too close—she would panic. She never left me alone with him for more than a few minutes. Even when she cooked a meal, she would be in and out of the kitchen to see what we were doing. I don't know why. She never said. It just disturbed her."

We were quiet for a minute. There were thoughts here that neither of us wanted to articulate, not about my father but about my mother's pathologically suspicious mind.

"I always found Nana very sneaky."

Ana paused to assess my reaction. My eyes were unflinchingly settled on hers.

"How so?" I asked.

"Remember the time you and Adèle went to Greece and you let me go with Nana and Papa to Scotland? You told her explicitly that you wanted me to see some of the countryside."

"I knew that if I didn't say something, she would just sit around at Great-Granny's in Easterhouse, that miserable dump."

Easterhouse was one of those bureaucratic disasters created to relocate a social mess called the Gorbals, one of the worst slums in the world, essentially transporting it from an old Glasgow neighbourhood to a new one. In a matter of months, the new looked depressingly like the old, something close to a battleground in Beirut. My grandmother, Jeannie McGregor, a widow now in her eighties, though she had never lived in the Gorbals, ended up in Easterhouse along with the hapless poor, the perpetually unemployed, football thugs, drug dealers, petty thieves, hookers, and who knows what else. She endured multiple break-ins and robberies, even though she had nothing of value to steal. Somehow she survived in both body and spirit.

"One day," Ana continued, "we went to the local shops near Great-Granny's house and saw some postcards of other towns. 'Let's get some,' Nana said, 'and send them to your daddy.'"

I was reminded of the intimations of my mother's manipulation of me as a child, a fact I had stubbornly resisted acknowledging as an adult. Ana seemed determined to change that.

"She wouldn't have taken me anywhere if I hadn't said anything to her about it. 'I'm going to tell my dad,' I said, 'that you never took me to any of these places.' You were the only one she was afraid to offend, the only one she would listen to."

I knew this, but it had long ago ceased to be a source of pride or pleasure for me. It had become something of a burden, my mother's oddball excesses always in need of curbing. Even as a young man, I frequently played the parent, she the child.

"We ended up going on only one trip outside Glasgow, to see Papa's dad, my great-grandfather. And she bribed me with candy and kisses not to tell you. I wanted to please her, I guess. But I felt guilty afterwards."

"Don't punish yourself for that, Ana. There's been enough guilt in this family to hang an army."

We laughed and shook our heads.

"I don't want to give you the wrong impression. I enjoyed going to Scotland, no question, but it was curious to see how Nana was more or less chained to the house. Her sole concern was to make sure Papa didn't drink. She didn't want Uncle Don and Papa to be alone. 'Watch he doesn't drink,' she would whisper to Don when he came to visit. Don would say, 'A wee beer won't do him any harm.' But Nana was obsessed with making sure he never touched the stuff. He was never left alone for any length of time. I saw this all the way through the trip and long afterwards."

Uncle Don was my mother's twin brother, a stocky, rough-hewn bricklayer who had been too young to fight in the last war. He held my father in reverence because he had survived it.

"It must have been tense," I said.

Ana nodded. "I had a good time, really, but Nana was never able to enjoy herself. She was always telling me who she liked and who she didn't—which was almost everybody we met, particularly Papa's relatives. Nana positively hated his stepsister, Dot."

Ana was moving quickly through the family tree. She was now referring to the family of my paternal grandfather, who had been a miner all his life. His wife had died when my father was just a toddler, and he had remarried into a full-blown family with two stepdaughters, Dot and Mary, and a stepson, Johnny.

"Do you know why Nana felt that way about Dot?" I asked.

"I have no idea. I was happy just to get the chance to see my great-grandfather. He looked so much like Papa—the long, hooked nose, the bony face, the warm eyes."

"It would have been a thrill for him to meet you, too," I said.

"He never took his eyes off me," she said.

"What did Nana do?"

"She was careful not to say anything when she was there, though she was always uptight in case Papa misbehaved. When they were back at Gran's place, she needled him constantly. She said cruel, humiliating things, calling him a drunk and an alcoholic, as if saying one thing was not enough. Sometimes this would develop into a fight. 'Shut up, woman!' he would bark. 'Ye dinna know what you're talkin' aboot!'"

Ana took a deep breath and sighed.

"Their life was always like this. I don't remember it any other way.

Always in a state of agitated tension. Nana didn't seem to realize how clearly I saw what she was doing: trying to make me hate Papa. 'Why are you so mean to him?' I used to ask her. 'I have to be,' she'd say. 'He's a drunken bum.' To her, it was a joke. 'I have to be mean to him to make sure he doesn't drink too much.'"

Ana looked at me, still worried that she was hurting me with the truth about my mother. But I was pained only by the cruelty my mother had inflicted on my father and by my inability to protect my daughter from the fallout.

"Papa was generally quiet. Most of what she said to him—she herself acknowledged this—went in one ear and out the other. Although," Ana added with a snort, "he was the one who used to rib her about him being Brains and her Nae Brains. She talked *at* him, never *with* him. I used to feel so sorry for him. I can still see him in my mind's eye, looking like a wounded puppy."

"She treated him the way she treated her cat."

"She was obsessed with that cat—almost as if it were a child. It was always hiding somewhere when I went to see her. I never remember cuddling that cat. What was its name?"

"Circe. You gave her that name," I reminded her.

"I did? Really?"

"Yes, when you were a little girl, Nana asked you to think up a name for her new kitten. Do you know where the name comes from? Ancient Greece. Circe was a sorceress who turned men and women into wild animals."

"That sounds about right. I just remember this big, fat, vicious, spitting creature pawing at me from under the chair."

"That cat modeled its behavior on hers."

"I think you're right," said Ana, laughing.

"I'm serious!" I said. "She was paranoid, and so was the cat."

"It never wanted to be held, but she held it anyway. She didn't hold it like an animal. She hung on to it like a doll she didn't want to lose, though it was always desperate to free itself. But she controlled and manipulated every minute of that poor animal's life. It was strange how it never turned on her the way it turned on other people. Maybe they needed each other."

We paused again, and I noticed my head shaking involuntarily. Even now, ten years later, my mother's behavior seemed incredible.

"The older I got, the more immature she seemed to become," Ana said. "She just got more and more bizarre. Eventually, I couldn't reason with her about anything. I once went to her place with Jenny, when we were about fifteen. You remember my friend Jenny, don't you? She didn't wear a lot of clothes in the summer and kinda showed off her body. Papa liked her and once cracked a joke that made the two of us laugh. That was too much for Nana, who didn't like him getting any attention, especially from another female. So she started to insult him until Jenny and I left, because we couldn't take anymore. The next time I saw Nana, she said, 'You shouldn't be hanging around with that girl.' I told her she was my good friend. 'I don't want that slut coming back here,' she said."

Slut, whore—I began to recall how my mother had used these terms all her life to express contempt for women who threatened her. Which was just about every woman she met.

"Nana's mistreatment of Papa got worse. Things were going missing, according to her—pounds of butter, cutlery, drinking glasses. She claimed Papa was carrying them off to his women in the building. This was long after he'd retired, but according to her, somebody or other he'd been 'gallivanting' with had stolen them. Poor Papa just sat there shaking his head."

Ana paused again. Now I was the one who sighed deeply and looked out the window. The clouds were unbroken across the sky.

"Are you okay?" she asked.

"I can't imagine why I didn't realize how serious their situation was."

"You were on sabbatical with Adèle in England, and I was staying with Alison and her family."

Alison was Ana's closest school friend. She had chosen to stay at her place under the supervision of her parents when I offered her the opportunity to take a year off school to travel around Europe with Adèle and me. I shouldn't have been too surprised that she didn't want to come with us. She was fifteen and seriously into boys, more so than I realized at the time.

"I can't help blaming myself," I said, "for being away from you and them at a time like this. Besides, the letters I received from your nana and papa were a dead giveaway. She kept repeating herself, and his handwriting progressively deteriorated. I remember mentioning this to Adèle. Mom kept saying the same things in every letter, and Dad said almost nothing at all. What he did write didn't sound like him."

"She probably told him what to say," Ana said. "She was the one who mailed the letters. He became just passive and immobile. He hardly said anything the last time I visited them. He just sat there with an exasperated look on his face, shaking his head at all her accusations."

"Did they ever go out around this time?"

"Alison's parents sometimes invited them over for dinner. I was always a bit uncomfortable with that. But Papa had a good time. Alison's brother-in-law had been in the army, so he and Papa talked about the war. Nana's interruptions couldn't spoil it, because there were others around to distract her. Otherwise—"

"It was bad then?"

"Bad," Ana replied emphatically. "Most of the time, she didn't let him carry on conversation at all. She talked over him, for him, at him, about him—and usually she didn't hold back in public. She'd frequently put him down when others were around. She had a reputation for being domineering—if not with her words, then with her looks or actions. The more agitated she became, the more passive he was. It took a lot to get anything out of him. He was mostly quiet and depressed."

Ana's face darkened. But she had a mission.

"The only time I got a chance to speak to him was when she was out of the room. The last time I was in their apartment on the Danforth, I managed to get him to say something when she'd gone down the hall for some reason. He spoke quickly and in a whisper: 'She went to the bathroom yesterday and couldn't open the door to get back out. She thought I had locked her in there and began screaming and pounding the walls. If you look in the door, you'll see a hole in the wall. That's where she put her fist through the plaster before I pulled the door open and let her out.'"

Tears were glistening in Ana's eyes. But she kept on.

"They were taking care of my transportation costs when you were away," she continued. "On the Sunday afternoon before you came back, Nana called to tell me they were bringing my subway tickets over because I hadn't come to pick them up. When they arrived, she came in with the tickets, and Papa just sat in the car. This was a bit unusual since the two of them already knew Alison's parents and had been to dinner twice. I ran out to the car to see what was wrong. He was sitting there in broad daylight, crying his eyes out. I'd never seen him like this before. I asked him what was wrong, but he wouldn't tell me. So I sat with him while Nana was inside chatting with Alison's mother. There was nothing I could do to comfort him."

As my daughter spoke, I thought about how far away physically and mentally I had been from all of this. What might have been possible had I been around, as I should have been, to help? I turned in my chair. Ana was aware of my growing discomfort.

"That was the last time I saw Papa," Ana said. "It was before Nana's hysterical phone call when you were back from Europe. 'I can't wake your papa up!' she's screaming into the phone. 'Have you called an ambulance?' I ask. 'I can't wake him up. He's taken some pills.' I yell at her to hang up the phone and call an ambulance, but she just keeps babbling. She hasn't heard a word I said. So I hang up and call the ambulance myself. And then I take off."

"I guess I arrived shortly after that," I said, recalling Adèle's alarmed face. "'Your dad's swallowed some pills,' she bawled. 'They've taken him to East General.' I just dropped my bags at the door and drove straight to the hospital."

"I was already there," Ana said. "The emergency room was like a bus station—bloody patients lying on stretchers in the hallways, nurses madly running around from one to the other. Papa had just had his stomach pumped and was sitting up in a cot, still trying to adjust his eyes to the surroundings. He grabbed my hand so hard and held on for dear life. It was the first time he ever showed me such affection. I kissed his cheek. 'I'm sorry, Ana,' he wailed. 'What for?' I said. 'For embarrassing you like this.' 'Papa,' I said, 'don't say that. Please.' But he kept muttering apologies. 'I love you, Ana. I didn't mean to hurt you.'

"For a man who wasn't used to sharing his feelings—someone who'd been so excessively withdrawn—he was extremely effusive. 'I love you, Papa,' I said, 'and I don't want you to go.' He smiled then, and I felt good about that. For the first time in my life, I thought I had broken through the barriers created by Nana between him and me. We held hands for a few minutes. I had the distinct impression that he was glad he hadn't succeeded in killing himself."

"Where was your nana?"

"She was standing behind me, wringing her hands, wearing those cheap sunglasses which had become a permanent fixture. She had this half-crazy look on her face. Then she did something so … so … ugly—I can't think of a better word—that it killed any respect or love I ever had for her."

Ana didn't try to hide her disgust.

"What happened?"

"She made a quick move at him, suddenly bumping me out of the way to lean forward into his face. It was as if his humiliation, his total misery, was not enough for her, and she was moving in for the kill. 'If you ever do this to me again,' she hissed, 'I'll just leave you there, you bastard.' She was so selfish, so vile! She viewed the whole thing as something he had done to her. He looked beaten. His eyes became dark; his whole face went dark. He just hung his head. I couldn't believe she had done this, and I didn't want him to believe it. I said, 'Everybody loves you, Papa. Don't listen to her.' He was withered and sick, down and out, and here she was kicking him in the stomach."

"Where was I?"

"You arrived right after this. Nana saw you coming, turned around, and smiled at you."

"I can still see the three of you in my mind's eye," I said. I felt like a complete fool—an incompetent fool, an impotent fool—for missing all this.

"I didn't know what to do. I was also a bit afraid. She looked vaguely dangerous. But my feelings for her changed right on the spot. I really believe that this, for Papa, was the final straw. She despised him. This is what I think led to his destruction. If she had expressed any affection for him—"

"I remember the look on his face when I came in," I interjected. "It was exactly as you say. If only I had known what your nana was doing." I shook my head in exasperation.

"I guess I should have told you, but I was stunned."

"You had an enormous burden to bear, Ana. You were so young!"

I was thinking here of not only all the incidents my daughter was describing but also the ones she was not describing. While Adèle and I were out of the country, Ana dropped out of high school before finishing grade twelve, found herself a job as somebody's secretary, and promptly got herself pregnant. All of this happened in the summer of '84, when I returned from Europe thinking I had cancer because I was in perpetual pain, and Adèle had to be rushed to hospital with a critical case of gallstones that had been misdiagnosed. I was thinking of all this as my daughter and I, at the same time, remembered what had occurred a few days after that, on the last day of May: my father's leap from the tenth-floor balcony of his apartment building. I remembered but didn't speak the last lines of the poem I had written about my old man that summer, "All His Life a Miner":

> Running with all his might
> in the largeness
> of his unlit days,
> he took a desperate plunge
> that brought him face-to-face
> with the lover
> he'd always courted,
> Endless Night,
> in the guise
> of an unmarked shaft,
> against the bottom of which
> he dashed
> his charcoal-smothered brains.

"After Papa died," Ana said, "Nana said things to me that I'll never forget. When I got pregnant, you and Adèle were out of town, and

I needed someone to talk to. I spent a couple of nights with her. She decided that I needed straightening out. 'You're a slut,' she said to me, 'but we can fix you. Just because you're one now doesn't mean you have to be a slut all your life.'"

I did some more squirming in my seat. I was beginning to feel really disgusted—not just with my mother but also with myself.

"'I made a mistake,' I said to Nana, 'but that doesn't make me a slut.' She said, 'I'm not blaming you,' but she was—if not for the pregnancy, then for what, in her mind, led to it. 'I told you hanging around with that girl'—Jenny—'would do you no good. But don't worry. I can show you how to be a lady again.'"

"It sounds a little surreal," I said, shaking my head. "Someone suffering from paranoia giving advice on moral rectitude."

"It was a nightmare. I lost all sense of connection with Nana. I just became detached. Numb."

I got up from my chair. It had become too uncomfortable to sit. I switched to small talk and made some tea, which we both needed. Then we continued.

"You realize, Ana, that Alzheimer's had taken possession of Nana's brain."

As soon as I said this, I could barely believe what I'd just said. Here I was, feebly trying to excuse my mother again. It was becoming more and more apparent, though, that this was not just Alzheimer's. Something else was going on, something that predated the dementia. Young Bobbie's comment was ringing in my ears: "Nana wasn't evil." Though I'd never thought she was evil, something screwy seemed to be happening long before the dementia.

"I realize what you're saying," Ana replied, "and I think I realized it then. But this had no effect on how I came to feel about her. Besides, she was only an exaggerated version of what she had been earlier, at least during my lifetime. Where did Nan's 'normal' personality end and the Alzheimer's take over?"

Her question was unanswerable. Even as a boy, I could remember always feeling embarrassed about my mother's peculiarities. I had long been uncertain whether these oddities were just a function of a child's natural sensitivities or whether they had been the early symptoms of something else, something that had occurred earlier in my mother's life that I knew nothing about—at this point.

"From the time I was a little girl," Ana continued, "I never really got to know Papa, because there was so much space between us. Who was to blame for that? It was more than ten years before Nana was diagnosed with Alzheimer's. When he told me stories about the war, she either stopped him or sent me to bed. He was never included in things. He was always on the outside. I remember a snapshot of me feeding a deer, with him standing behind me and smiling. I missed seeing that smile at the time. I hardly remember him smiling at all. I'm so disappointed that I didn't get to know him. I feel I let him down. I never believed all those things about him, but I never defended him. He was not to be trusted, according to her, though never once did he do anything remotely inappropriate around me. I was simply supposed to avoid being close to him.

"What was Nana trying to punish him for? God knows. 'He adores you,' she used to say, all the while manipulating me in order to hurt him.

"I watched her doing this so many times. 'He's had a drink today,' she would tell me when I visited. 'Don't go near him.' She would then make sure that I didn't get too affectionate with him. This was his punishment for misbehaving. He was always getting beat up for doing anything sociable. She'd just shoot him down. Once he playfully put his pipe in my mouth, and she flew into a rage. He never had any fun. When it looked like he might, she would be furious."

Ana looked at me worriedly. I had told her I wanted the truth, but she didn't want to hurt me with it. At this point, I was stricken by the realization that what my mother had done to Ana—manipulating her feelings about my father—she had previously done to me. We had both been caught in the same ever-widening vortex.

"Are you okay?" she asked.

"I'm fine," I said, trying to hide my horror. "Please go on with the rest of your story."

"I went over to see her a few times after her comments about my being a slut, but only out of a sense of obligation, more toward you than her. She was friendly enough. She'd forgotten all the things she had said to me. She wasn't eating, and the cat was starving. I would make her dinner and sit and talk for a while. Her stories were bizarre. Everything was a conspiracy. Some people in the building she lived in at the time were trying to get her, she said. According to her, they were coming into the apartment when she was out or asleep, and they were taking silverware, jewelry, clothing, drinking glasses, food—anything.

"Once I asked her if there was any butter for the potatoes I'd made for our supper. She went to the freezer and didn't find it there. I was sorry I asked, because she spent the next half hour looking around the house for it, complaining that somebody had robbed her. When I joked that no one would come into her apartment to steal butter, she was not amused. She drove herself into a frenzy over how it had gone missing, who took it, why this was happening to her, what she would do to the person when she got hold of her, et cetera.

"I'd often go looking for things myself, until I realized that she had either not bought whatever she was hunting for or that she'd hidden it to keep it safe from the people who were out to steal it from her and then forgotten where she put it. I once found her reading glasses in with the pots and pans, and her cutlery under the bed."

We laughed ruefully at the circus our memories conjured up.

"I found a half dozen liquor bottles in 'secret' locations when she moved out of that apartment," I said. "One or two empties, a couple of full ones. Maybe another two or three half full."

"Really?" Ana cried with a bitter laugh. "You mean she was actually drinking?"

"Yes. Quite heavily."

"That's so ironic after the way she used to go after Papa."

"People do strange things when they're desperate."

"She was always trying to give me things," Ana went on. "Trinkets, knick-knacks, plastic necklaces, money. I didn't want them. Besides, I didn't want her turning on me the way she had turned on other people. She was always going on about how the other tenants in her building had turned against her. Sometimes when we were passing through the lobby, people milling around, she'd denounce the people she played bingo with or curse some woman as 'the one who's stealing' such and such. She hated most women as far as I could see and feared all men. Nana used to avoid an old guy in a wheelchair even though he joked about it with her. 'Don't speak to him,' she'd whisper to me, 'even if he speaks to you.'"

"She was terribly lonely, Ana. And pathologically afraid."

"But she brought it on herself! She alienated everyone around her. Drove people away."

I knew Ana was right, and I was aghast at how I had compulsively excused my mother. I thought that she surely didn't know what she was doing. Mom had succumbed to the dementia of Alzheimer's at a relatively early age, or something else that was never diagnosed at an even earlier age. She couldn't understand why everything she touched seemed to disappear or why all her friends and neighbours began to avoid her. I had begun to receive phone calls that she was wandering in the middle of the night. Once I found the large burner on her stove turned on full blast when she was out of the apartment. The risks outweighed the benefits of her living by herself. Eventually, I managed to persuade her to go to the hospital, where she would undergo tests and eventually be diagnosed as an Alzheimer's patient.

I thought all these things, but Ana wasn't convinced, and her story sowed doubts where none had existed before. Perhaps she was right. Perhaps my mother had always been a manipulator. Maybe she was just off her rocker.

"I didn't realize how bad she had become," Ana recollected, "until the weekend Les and I took her up to Muskoka."

Les was Ana's first live-in boyfriend, whom she eventually married and subsequently divorced after a short-lived partnership.

"I had been so proud," she went on, "of owning a cottage that I wanted to show it off to my grandmother. All the way up in the car, she kept asking me when we would get there. And every five minutes, I would tell her it's a long way. When we got there, the first night was hell. She woke us up screaming in the middle of the night. 'Someone was peering in the window at me,' she insisted. Our assurances weren't enough, and she went to sleep with a flashlight in her hand. Two minutes later, after

Les and I had gotten back into bed, she was yelling again. I eventually got into bed with her and cuddled her the whole night long."

"She had become a baby again."

"During the day, she wasn't so bad. She enjoyed listening to the loons and watching the ducks on the lake. But the trip back to Toronto was another nightmare. Halfway there, she began to say she didn't want to go back to the hospital. As we got closer to the city, she grew more desperate. She began to whimper, 'I don't want to go back there. Just take me home.' 'Nana,' I said, 'you can't go home. There's no one there to look after you.' But she just became more insistent. 'I'll give you all my money,' she said. 'Just let me off here.' 'You'll never survive,' I said, stupidly still trying to reason with her. 'On the streets of Toronto? C'mon!'"

"Strangely enough, she did understand that she was trapped," I said. "She blamed everybody else—you, me, the hospital staff—for keeping her locked up, of course, but her perception that there was no way out was right. She was locked into Alzheimer's by then."

"When we pulled up at the front door of the hospital, she turned on me and shocked the hell out of Les. The simpering child suddenly morphed into a tiger with an abscess in its tooth. 'You're disgusting, mean, horrible!' she snarled. 'You don't care about me. You never loved me. You just want to send me to my doom.' Luckily, she had no physical strength left; otherwise, she'd have been hard to handle. As it turned out, she came quietly with me back to her room. After everyone welcomed her back, she began to feel better, I guess. She underwent another transformation, and I couldn't believe it was the same person. She thanked me for the lovely weekend, for being so good to her, and she kissed me half a dozen times before I left, telling me each time how much she loved me."

My daughter's words, so carefully selected and apt, were still not enough to convey the ferocity of spirit we had both encountered in this woman we had once loved and known so well—a spirit that had been consumed by demons and grown into something quite monstrous. If Ana had been unable to shed her youthful resentment about how this affected her papa, I was incapable of shaking off the enormous guilt I felt about my own lack of foresight and my inaction. Had I ever really known my mother? Had I ever really known myself, given that I had been so deluded by her chicanery? Maybe she had always been a stranger to me. Maybe I had always been a stranger to myself.

Ana and I sat together for a while after this conversation in a kind of mute paralysis, looking out my window across the lake. We could see a storm gathering. It was coming this way.

"I should get home before the weather breaks," she said.

"I'll walk with you," I replied. "I need some air."

5
Mother's Day

It's Mother's Day, and I bring her chrysanthemums—yellow chrysanthemums. But the nurses have turned her round so that she is facing away from the window where I want to place the flowers. Her eyes are open. I position myself in her line of vision. Is there a flicker of recognition? She stares, as usual, without comprehension. The edges of her eyelids are encrusted, and her lips are caked with dried skin. Like a child, she sticks her tongue out to lick her lips. Her cheeks are sunken in against the bones. Her grey hair is pulled up into the ponytail she would have abhorred had she known who she was.

She tries to squeeze some sounds out of her withered lungs but cannot articulate them into words. She retreats into silence and closes her eyes when I stroke her head.

The Kangaroo feeder suddenly begins to beep like the back-up alarm on a truck. I jump, and a pained, quizzical expression creases my mother's forehead.

A nurse comes in.

"Excuse me," she says. She pushes a button to silence the Kangaroo. "I'll be right back to fill it up."

As soon as she leaves, the machine begins to beep again. My mother grimaces with her eyes tightly shut. Is she in pain? Or is it just irritation? I clasp her hand and kiss her cheek. She opens her eyes. I make funny faces, acting like the child I become in her presence. They hold her attention for a few minutes. Her frown disappears, but only momentarily.

The nurse comes back to fill up the feeder, at the same time calling out instructions to someone outside the room. I take a break. I have to squeeze through the room's doorway past a man wearing diapers. His pants hang down around his knees. Another man, a Chinese man with a near-beatific smile on his face, saunters along beside me in his pyjamas as if he were my constant companion. In the background, I hear a woman wailing like a lost child.

When I wind my way back into my mother's room, Mrs. Mohammed, on the other side, is lying on her back, staring at the ceiling with a look of panic in her eyes. Her long black hair is spread out like a horse's mane on the pillow. Her husband comes in, yells at her in Hindi so that she can understand him, and pats her on the shoulder to get her attention.

The lady in the bed beside my mother's, Mrs. Garceau, sits up. She coughs and splutters and takes a sip of juice. Stares at me blankly and decisively lies back down again.

"Happy Mother's Day," I whisper to my mother as I lean forward to look into her eyes, which recognize nothing.

Against the backdrop of noise, unpredictable beeps, loud chatter, and echoing screams, my mother's silence is striking. Not just her ability to speak but also the basic human—animal—trait of making sounds using her throat has all but disappeared.

Her lips, at their corners, seem to be sealed together. Perhaps all her orifices are beginning to close up. I ponder whether it is to close *over* or close *out* the emptiness. Why is she hanging on only to endure all this pain and misery? Is there something she still has to do, or is it all just instinctive? Does she fear letting go? Or is it the habit of holding on? My Zen monk, who usually pops up when I have these questions, doesn't seem to have heard me today. Maybe he's lost interest.

I look out the window at the endless buzz of traffic on the freeway below. On the baseball diamond, kids like ants dart back and forth. The sun creeps round from behind the hospital at an agonizingly slow pace. The perpetual brown haze hangs over the cluster of downtown buildings in the distance.

This is what occurs—nothing more, nothing less. Life trundles on. Death seeps in through the cracks.

6

Not from Fine China

M aggie Glascoe was becoming far stranger to me than she had started out to be. She wasn't a hard woman for me to love, for obvious reasons, but I was finding it more and more difficult to justify her increasingly bizarre behavior. Her relationships with those closest to her were the most troublesome, including those with her daughters-in-law. My second wife, Adèle, was by far the best at handling my mother and less sanguine about the wounds my mother inflicted.

Adèle, who had been born in Guyana—or British Guiana, as it was known at the time of her birth—came to Canada as a student and never left. A strikingly beautiful woman of mixed race, she had the ink-black hair, dark almond-shaped eyes, and unblemished skin from her Indian origins and the slightly hooked nose and supple limbs of her North African ancestors. Adèle combined practical intelligence and moral strength with a desire to fit in and make her mark. She was curious and careful, thoughtful and loyal. A woman of strong character, she was a good judge of the same in others. Adèle and I met on a train, purely by chance.

We belonged to the tradition, established in the '60s, of honeymooning before the wedding, having lived together in blissful sin for several years before we were married. Adèle moved in with Ana and me after we returned from hitchhiking across Canada. She managed the role of the stepmother with a growing child hurt by her parents' recent divorce with consummate sensitivity and skill. Adèle was remarkably sensitive to my daughter's need to heal the relationship with her biological mother yet remained open to becoming Ana's alternate or second mother.

"Do you remember," I asked Adèle, "when you first met my mother?"

"My first impression of your mom is the one that lasted throughout the time I knew her. She was just doing what was expected of her. I don't know why I felt that way, but it seemed to me that with your father, you, and Ana, she was doing what she had to do. I don't know what she might have been anticipating when I came into the picture, but she didn't show any surprise at what I looked like or at my race. She knew that she had to do right by you. Ana and you were the most important people in her life."

"What did she say to you? How did she treat you?"

"In those early days, she didn't say anything to offend me, if that's what you mean. She was polite, never uncivil."

"How did my father respond?"

"Your father warmed to me immediately. The first time I met him was when we visited them at their place. He showed a genuine interest in me. He loved my hair, which, at that time, was a mass of curls. I remember him asking, 'Where did you get all those curls?'"

"He knew you were mainly Indian, and having been to India himself, he knew Indians have mainly straight hair."

"And mine was too, but after I met you, I changed the style. Your dad welcomed me; your mother was so unnatural. *He* made me feel at home; *she* treated me like a guest. That was okay, but there was a real difference. When I think of her, certain words come to mind."

"Such as?"

"*Pretentious. Affected.* I knew from you that your family was working class, but when I met her, I knew she was trying to make an impression. She was superficial and artificial. She didn't come from fine china, but she liked to pretend she did."

I didn't have to worry about asking Adèle to be candid. She had a remarkable ability to balance the observations of her keen eye with a sensitivity about their effects.

"The other words are *intelligent* and *strong*. She was loyal, too, but only to her immediate family. You were everything to her, a grown man who she treated like a boy."

There it was again—the same refrain Ana had uttered: my mother's obsession with me. Her love was the overindulgent manipulation that went far beyond the boundaries of a healthy relationship—a love that rarely gave me any comfort. It was mostly a burden to me—a deeply possessive, ingratiating love.

"She was charming," Adèle added, "or maybe it's better to say she knew how to turn on the charm. I'm not sure, but Maggie may have been a flirt in her youth."

"That's probably an understatement."

"And she was openly contemptuous of what she didn't understand," Adèle said, then immediately turned things around to balance the picture: "But she was a really good cook. Excellent, in fact."

"It was pretty basic Scotch fare."

"Yes, but she knew how to do it to perfection. Her steak and sausage pies were fantastic."

My mother knew how to make puff pastry better than a chef did. She had worked for years in the catering business and knew what good dining was and how to prepare a banquet for VIPs. She had once worked in the High Park Curling Club, where I'd seen one of her spreads for a special occasion. I had been stunned. I'd had no idea that her work was so classy. Adèle valued this kind of skill.

"How did my mother treat you when she learned we were getting married?"

"One day, some time before the wedding, I was at your parents' house alone. You had gone to pick up Ana. There was some sort of in-house yard sale on downstairs in their building, and your mom wanted to go for a look. She thought she should go alone, and put it in such a way as to protect me. 'I don't want them to say anything to upset you, Adèle.' She apologized for leaving me alone, though your dad was there. This is the only time I recall that she ever said anything that related to race."

"She made it sound as if she were protecting you," I added, "but she was protecting herself."

"Exactly. She didn't have to explain anything. But you know, that remark slid off me then."

"Though you still remember it now."

"Yes. But there was nothing of this when we told her about the wedding. We were sitting on the porch of the Lee Avenue house. She and your dad were down there every weekend. She didn't say she was happy we were getting married but said, 'Oh, good, you're not going to be living together anymore!' That was fine—I felt something genuine was coming from her then. And when we told her the date had been set for July twelfth, again I felt the same thing. She knew I was Catholic, so she didn't think it was a good idea to get married on Orangemen's Day."

Though the Orangemen's Parade was still held in Toronto in 1980, when Adèle and I were about to marry, fewer and fewer people in Canada celebrated the historical "triumph" of Protestants over Catholics. But it had been serious business in the life of my family before they left Scotland. My mother, occasionally, had taken me as a child to the Orange Walk, mainly because it was a street party. Her best friends in my childhood were her Catholic neighbours across the street, people she'd known for twenty years and who treated me like their own son. So the Orange Walk for me as an adult was just idiotic nonsense.

Adèle broke into my reverie. "Anyway, this made me feel good. She was acting like a typical parent. She also asked about my parents. Were they happy to hear the news? Are they coming to the wedding? We also talked about the arrangements, since you and I had decided to perform the ceremony at home. She got involved in this. I liked that. She was extremely competent on that score. She knew how to plan and what to cook for a wedding."

"She was an expert at this stuff."

"I never felt uncomfortable with that. In fact, I was glad of the help. We wanted something Scottish. I knew she did great hams and steak pies, so we went with that and some other stuff I suggested. But she couldn't stomach turkey or chicken or any birds at all. It was the carcass that troubled her."

"What happened when your mom arrived?"

This was a key issue, because my mother-in-law-to-be, Cecile, was just like my mother, in more ways than one. She was a strong-minded, no-nonsense kind of lady with class pretensions that probably exceeded my mother's. Strangely enough, Maggie and Cecile did not have to be monitored to keep them from coming to blows.

"Jurisdictions were determined," Adèle noted. "They took care of separate things. Your mom was in control of all the entrees; my mom was in charge of the sweet things, mostly the cake, which was a grand affair. It was fun to watch the two of them working together in our kitchen in the days leading up to the wedding. I was always surprised at how well your mother dealt with that."

"I was surprised at how well your mother handled it," I said. "You'd warned me about the authoritarian streak in her personality."

"I think it worked because both our mothers were both so loyal to their children."

Adèle's remark reminded me of how perfectly these two women understood each other. Their cooperation had played such a big part in making the wedding day a happy and memorable one for all of us.

"After we were married," Adèle continued, "your mom came over to visit us a lot. She was alone during the day because your dad worked nights. I think she liked the way our place looked, the way I dressed, so she wanted to go shopping with me. She wanted new stuff—dresses, coats, shoes. She tried things on that she liked and that I thought looked really good on her. Then she'd say, 'I don't think Bob would like this.' I was surprised to hear her say that, considering the way she treated him. She was so coarse, harsh, impatient—so intolerant when it came to dealing with him. I never saw any real love there. On the other hand, he was her man, and she took care of him in other ways. She dutifully packed his lunch—a big whopper of a lunch, as I remember it. Made sure all his clothes were ready for him when he got up to go to work."

"There were a lot of contradictions in their relationship."

"She and I were having coffee one time on Queen Street in the Beaches. I don't know how your dad came up in the conversation, but she started to complain about him. She said, 'I should have left him a long time ago.' She was in her sixties then, and I was shocked that she actually said this to me. The way she went on about it, though, indicated that she now just accepted the situation as her lot in life. This conversation helped me to be more tolerant of her. I knew she was carrying a lot inside."

Adèle always amazed me with her statesmanlike capacity for dealing with difficult family relationships. She wasn't always as cool headed with her own mother, but perhaps because she had come through some rough times with a tough, authoritarian matriarch, she understood the value of moderation and balance in family life. Our own relationship was hardly exemplary, but I have to admit that it wasn't for the want of her efforts. Our early years together had been good, but Adèle and I, at the time of this conversation, had been together for some twenty-odd years. It had not all been sweetness and light. I had encouraged her to go back to university for a second degree in nutrition, with the hope that she would move out of the "medical industry," as I contemptuously referred to it, because of the its failures in the case of my own health.

In spite of my recriminations, after graduating from her second stint at university, she had gone to work in the pharmaceutical industry. For me, this was like going from the fireplace into the furnace, and it remained a bone of contention between us for years, along with all the travelling she was required to do as part of the job. We fell into a pattern of grating on each other's nerves. I reacted impulsively and angrily to situations like this and got involved with other women. To Adèle, I seemed to have become just another womanizer, but now I think these extramarital relationships were just a symptom of an ongoing depression that I barely noticed, a depression that probably evolved from my family history, though I can't and don't lay it all at the feet of my parents. I was volatile and obdurate and became increasingly so as the acrimony between Adèle and me increased. Yet we hung on to each other for years to come.

"Your mom used to infuriate me," she said, "by telling Ana a lot of old wives' tales. She told her once not to wash her hair when she was having her period and not to have a bath in case she might get pregnant."

This was one of those anecdotes that made me wonder about my mother's sanity. Ana's question popped into my head again: When did my mother's Alzheimer's really begin? Adèle was aware of my sudden discomfort, and she switched to another topic.

"Your mom and I actually had some good times together. I took her to see Tom Jones. I liked him, but she was *crazy* about the man! A whole different woman was with me at that concert. We had second-row seats, centre stage. She was whooping it up and waving her arms in the air like a bird frantically flapping its wings after being suddenly uncaged. Almost all the women in the audience were silver haired and the same age as your mother, but they looked as if they were ready to tear Tom Jones's clothes off—your mother included. They threw flowers and underwear at him. Your mom dug something out of her purse—I don't know what it was—and tossed it right onto the stage. Remember that song "She's a Lady"? God, you should have seen her! I can still here her singing along with Tom Jones at top of her lungs while she danced in the aisle: 'Well, she's all you'd ever want … ' I never saw anything like it!"

I cringed at the thought but marveled at Adèle's efforts, which I had long forgotten about, to connect with my mother.

Adèle continued. "I also took her to see the Alvin Ailey dancers. It wasn't quite the same for her. She enjoyed going, but I don't think she understood it. They were all black, of course, but I don't think it was just that. It was contemporary ballet and a far cry from Tom Jones. I'm glad I took her, though. It showed her a bit more of me and the things I liked."

"Not long after this," I said, "we spent that year in Europe. A lot was happening then."

"I thought we were going to break up," Adèle said. Her face had fallen. "You'd come back in March; I stayed on until the middle of April. You left me an ominous note."

"You were ill; I was ill," I said to excuse myself. "Ana was pregnant, and my parents were in some kind of trouble I didn't understand at the time."

"You wrote more letters before I came home and seemed to back off from breaking up, and then I arrived home."

"Distance puts some things in perspective," I said. "So does other people's suffering."

"You were worried about your dad. He was constantly saying that everything was junk. I had the impression even before I came home that he was fed up with life. When I first went to visit them in their tiny retirement apartment, though, he was happy to see me. Maybe it was a relief to have us back, to get her off *his* back. He seemed glad to have someone else there. He made Scotch broth."

"He was still doing that then?"

"Their roles had kind of reversed. Your mom seemed a bit incapacitated, though I didn't know what was wrong. Anyway, he was doing more of the cooking. He said to me sort of mockingly, 'She gets all excited because *Son* is coming today.' We seemed to be visiting them almost every weekend. You were also going over there during the week. My recollection is that your mom was not doing so well for some reason and that your dad was devoting a lot of time to looking after her. I didn't understand what her condition was, but I know she'd started with the purse thing—constantly hiding it and then panicking because she was unable to find it."

"You'd been home a little more than a month," I reminded her, "when that first alarm-bell phone call came from my mother. Ana picked it up."

"Yes, then I talked to her. I think she called from the hospital emergency room. She wasn't in what I would call a hand-wringing state. I guess by that time, your dad was okay. She just told me that he'd been rushed to hospital. You just kicked into gear."

"She was incapable by then."

"I remember you being very involved. You saw them every day. You arranged medical tests for your dad, and you went with him."

"How did you feel when he died?" I asked her. "I don't remember."

"I was shocked by how he died. It was very sad for me. I cared about your dad. But I was also worried about you; I was really disappointed that you wouldn't allow me to comfort you through all of that. You pushed me away—so much so that I didn't really want to go to the funeral. I didn't feel that I was part of your life then. You were showing very little emotion. I understood that—you had so much to do; you were the one who had to take care of all the arrangements around his death. But I knew you were hurting, and I was hurting too because you wouldn't share it with me.

"That changed my whole feeling about you after that. Mind you, I wasn't well myself, so I was feeling a little vulnerable. Even at the funeral home, you lifted my hand off your arm and moved it away. It showed me a side of you I'd never seen before. I think it's something you do to deal with pain."

I wasn't aware that I had done it, and I'm not sure what it was all about. Maybe Adèle was right. When I think of it, I had in the past turned away from relatives and friends when our relationships became too difficult.

"I saw it again when I had the surgery later that summer," she added.

"That would have been the 'summer of hell' in '84." I was beginning to recall all kinds of events I'd sooner have forgotten.

"You were trying to take care of all of us that summer. You had a lot to carry. I know all this now, but then I was hurting. Do you remember the hospital calling you?"

"I think so. There was an urgent phone call at one point."

"After I'd had the operation to remove my gallstones, I woke up in the middle of the night with nurses and doctors all around me. I had a fever, and they were worried about an infection in the operated area. I had to pull through that fever if I was going to live."

This painful memory reasserted itself. The surgeon had told us afterward that he'd thought he was going to lose my beautiful Adèle.

Adèle's family doctor was an old university friend who had a drinking problem. Adèle was used to discussing minor medical issues with her friend over the phone. On this occasion, the doctor had misdiagnosed the gallstones, thinking the symptoms indicated jaundice or some such thing. The result had been a delay in getting Adèle to hospital. By the time I'd decided I wasn't going to wait any longer for her practitioner to sober up and get her ducks in place, Adèle had been doubled over in pain, and her abdomen had been swollen like a balloon. I'd carried her downstairs to the car and rushed her to the hospital. She had been there barely a couple hours before the doctors decided to operate.

"You told me afterwards that you went home and sat at the dining table, preparing for me to die. You called everybody—my brother, sister, and cousin in London—to let them know. They all called me, worried out of their minds."

"I was devastated. I was kicking myself for not taking you to the emergency a lot sooner. You wanted to wait for your doctor to give the go-ahead. I knew that was a mistake, because you were getting more and more critical."

"As it turned out," Adèle added with the characteristic humor she often showed in difficult moments, "there I was—three floors up, in the same hospital as my stepdaughter, Ana, who was giving birth to her child!"

I was glad for the conversation's change in direction.

"One day, when I was still in the hospital convalescing but able to stand up by the window, I saw you walking through the parking lot with a baby in your arms."

"That was Ana's baby. I'd arranged for him to be adopted, and I had to take him to Sick Kids Hospital for the transfer."

"I was admiring your ability to step in and focus then. Those were such strange times."

I didn't feel particularly admirable that day. I was in constant pain. I had lost a lot of weight and was unable to get a diagnosis from mainstream doctors that made any sense to me. I was carrying on with my own self-medicating alternative therapy. It provided only short bursts of relief, and I thought I might not live much longer. Neither I nor Adèle was able to take care of a baby, which is what I thought we would have to do, since Ana had done nothing to demonstrate that she understood the kind of responsibility needed for the job. She wanted to keep the child, but she was repeatedly playing hooky from school and finally dropped out at sixteen years old, while keeping the pregnancy to herself until it was too late to do anything about it. She seemed oblivious to anything beyond her own plight and couldn't imagine that there was anything to my decision but an assertion of blunt authority. Given the state of health both Adèle and I were in, I didn't care what she thought; I was just glad I still had the legal power to do what I did. It was painful to remember this now. I changed the subject.

"Do you remember my mom coming to visit you in the hospital?"

"No. I remember others but not her."

"I brought her in a couple of times."

"I know that when I got out of the hospital, we saw her a lot. You would go and fetch her. She brought me soup a few times when I was still unable to eat solid food."

Around this time, Mom was hospitalized for extensive testing and diagnosis. It turned out as I had expected: she had Alzheimer's disease. After my father's death, I investigated a number of homes for the aged. They were all horrible, not because the people who worked in them were a bad lot—just the opposite, in fact. The problem was the institutionalization of the aged and dying—packing all the elderly together and, in the case of those like my mother, all the demented on one floor. The general misery was apparent and appalling.

"Your mom stayed over a lot for the next year or two, even after she was settled into the Dawes Road home. I wasn't around much, because I was back at university. When Ana eventually turned eighteen, she found her own place, and we moved into a one-bedroom apartment to save money. Your mother got steadily worse, and your relationship with her changed. I came home from school one day to hear you screaming at her on the phone."

I still felt ashamed when Adèle reminded me of this, but I was the only one who took any responsibility for her care. My brother and his family lived out of town and offered no direct help. Ana seldom went to see her, and when she did, it was more for my sake than her nana's. I was her only regular visitor, though sometimes Adèle accompanied me. But as her condition worsened, I was pushed to my limits.

One day, after I took her out for a walk in the park next to her residence, she refused to go back inside. We were on the street, and she pulled away from me. I was hesitant about using any force in a public place; people might think I was molesting her. She was crying her eyes out as she trundled along the street—a truly pathetic sight. She stopped at a bus shelter and just stood there, determined not to budge. I stomped off in exasperation, leaving her, I thought, to get lost. But I couldn't go through with it and ran back to the shelter to find her, thankfully, still there. She was sobbing about having nowhere to go. This was one of the lowest moments we shared. I knew that in spite of her growing dementia, she was profoundly unhappy because she knew full well what was happening.

"I remember her brother Don coming here to see her," Adèle said. "After that, she just became less competent and had to be moved to higher and higher floors in the residence for more intensive care. There were a lot of West Indians working on her floor, and one of the last coherent things I remember your mother saying—to Ana, not to me— was that they were 'Adèle's people.'"

Adèle's story wound down to a full stop. She didn't really know much about my mother in her last years, at least from direct contact. Mom was transferred from the home for the aged to Riverdale Hospital, where I was her only regular visitor.

The fragile bond between them had been broken.

7
The Madman

Sometimes when I visit my mother, there's a madman with me—the one who walks in my shadow most of the time. I just can't shake him off. He's relentless in his efforts to pester me and knows everything I'm thinking. He voices all the anger and cruelty bottled up inside me, ready to explode at a moment's notice. Today when I take her head in my hands, he whispers viciously in my ear.

"Why don't you just wring her neck?"

"What the hell are you going on about?"

"You keep wondering why she's hanging on like this, why she endures all this suffering—the pain, the disease, et cetera."

"So?"

"So just give her neck a quick, hard twist. Now. Try it. A little jerk will be enough to snap the brittle old bones."

"Beat it, will you?"

"Don't plead with me to go. You know as well as I do why I'm here. You invited me."

"I don't want to cause her any more pain than she already endures. Don't you understand that?"

"Breaking her neck would be the last pain she'd ever feel. A little agony to end all the agony. Go on—give it a go."

"Get lost!"

But at times like this, he never does. He needles me to distraction with his comments about my weakness and drives me to despair.

"You're a nobody," he says. "A nothing. *Nihil ex nihilo*—nothing comes from nothing." He sniggers, pointing at my mother.

I hold my old lady's head in my hands, longing for some kind of communion with her. She stares back, oblivious to my plight. Without warning, she clenches her toothless jaws, yawns in my face with the abandon of an infant, and slowly closes her eyes. She falls once more into a semi-comatose state.

Behind my back, I hear the bellowing laughter of the madman as he exits the scene. He's enjoying the mayhem he just caused.

8
Dinner at the Lido

What was so compelling about the search I'd undertaken was that the stories I heard from each of my family members recounted the same patterns of events from different angles—the ever-widening circle of suffering my mother had caused and endured, a circle that never completed itself. Each one told a single story, converging in some details and diverging in others, about the same person. Or was it the same person? The more I learned about her, the less I seemed to know about my mother.

My first wife, Maria, always called her Maggie. I'd kept in touch with Maria since we divorced in what now seemed another lifetime. She was then living with a man named Joe. I sometimes saw them at family gatherings. We were good friends, as ex-spouses can be after they've had a child together and broken up. We'd been so young all those years ago, pressured by our parents into marrying because Maria was expecting a baby. It was hardly a forced marriage, but she and I were pushovers for ardent parents who colluded to make it happen.

It wasn't by any means an unhappy marriage, though there were some rough moments. When I met her, Maria was gentle, unassuming, unformed, even timid, and I wanted to try everything, to change the world, to go everywhere and break all the rules. We were very different people and perhaps incompatible from the beginning, but we loved and cared for each other. Eventually, we grew apart, and the differences between us became too great for me to ignore. When I left in the seventh year of our marriage, it devastated Maria, Ana, and even me. Ana ran away from Maria a few times, distraught because she thought that the breakup was Maria's fault. The three of us agreed that Ana would be better off living with me. As it turned out, this arrangement worked best. Over time, the blaming stopped, and Ana and Maria repaired their relationship. Eventually, Maria even accepted Adèle.

When I decided to speak to Maria about my mother, more than thirty years had intervened. Both her mother and Joe had died prematurely, and she had suffered a mild stroke. I didn't have much hope that she would recall a lot, but she had known my mother when she was still in charge of her faculties. I was hoping that she might have memories of the woman my mother was.

"I don't remember much," she warned me before we got under way.

I didn't want to be stalled that easily. "Do you recall first meeting her?"

"I guess it was '65, just after we were going out together. She and your dad were having a New Year's Eve party. There were a lot of people there. She seemed so outgoing then. I don't remember much of that party," she said with laugh, "but there were a lot of Scotch people bringing in bits of coal."

"The Scotch do odd things at New Year's. They carry coal over the threshold for good luck."

"That was the only time I remember her having friends over," Maria said, growing thoughtful. "She seemed to change after that. She turned more solitary. You became the most important thing in her life."

It was the same old refrain again—me. I don't know why I didn't pursue this comment with Maria. I know it was a bone of contention, almost an indictment, although there was no hint of this in her voice. Maria had great difficulty saying anything unkind to anyone and avoided confrontations like the plague. But my mother's inability to fault her two sons for anything was itself a fault in her relationship with her daughters-in-law.

"I remember your dad better than your mom." Her voice changed when she spoke of my father. She smiled warmly as she recollected something he had said to her. "When he found out I was expecting, he thought it was the responsible thing to do—get married."

"He actually said that to you?"

"Yeah, those were his words."

Maria and I, in the heady days of the mid-'60s, were still innocents and, despite our long hair, multi-colored shirts, bell-bottom pants, and long necklaces, only made it to the fringes of hippiedom. When she missed her period after our first forays into sex, she went to see a doctor who lectured her on the ethics of illegitimacy and told her she wasn't pregnant. We soon found out what a colossal mistake that had been. Maria was successful in hiding the fact from our parents for months. When it got to the point where we could no longer hide it, disclosure was difficult. As it turned out, our parents were pretty good about it. Maria's mother had given birth to two so-called illegitimate children herself, and my parents seemed unfazed by the prospect.

"I remember Dad saying one night," I told Maria, "after he had a drink, of course, that I could 'bring the wee baby over here to stay'—to the one-bedroom apartment they and I were living in at the time! Can you imagine? God only knows what we were all thinking in those strange times. Do you remember what led up to us getting married?"

"No. It just seemed to happen all of a sudden. I was in the hospital, having the baby. Next thing I knew, I was getting married. I'm sure there was a lot going on between the parents."

"I'll say. Who in hell would have chosen to perform a marriage ceremony with the bride still on the hospital bed right after bearing a child? We were still kids!"

Maria laughed. It had been a long time ago, and all the pain was, at least for now, forgotten. The absurd comedy remained.

"I know my mother had a lot to do with it," I confessed, "because the minister was a Presbyterian."

"Did we go to see him?"

"Yes, don't you remember that?"

"No. The only things I remember are from the photos."

I squirm when I think of those wedding photos—Maria still in her bedclothes, sitting up in the hospital bed with a blank look on her face, having given birth the day before, the minister solemnly standing on one side of the bed, me on the other with a red face. My brother, Robert, is looking moodily away from the camera. All the parents are lined up together with wooden smiles plastered on their faces.

"There was some legal technicality," I said, "about Ana not being able to have my name if we weren't married before she left the hospital. When I think of it now, that may well have been a fairy tale invented by my mother and yours to get us to the altar."

"So that's what the big rush was all about."

I didn't know Maria hadn't known that. How incredibly naive we had been. I wanted to move on from this—not because it was painful to remember but because I was embarrassed by the stupidity of the whole thing.

"We lived for a while on Lakeshore Road after that," I reminded her, "and I worked for a couple of years before I went to university."

"I remember the woman downstairs complained about the noise from Ana's walker on the floor. So we had to move, to an apartment a few doors away from your parents. Your mom was always there—I guess because she lived close by."

"Now I'm the one who's drawing a blank," I confessed. "I don't remember living next to them."

"Yeah, we lived in a building a few doors away from them. They eventually moved into an apartment upstairs from us in the same building."

"What? They lived that close?"

"Yes. They were around all the time then."

This sounded incredible to me. When I think of it, however, Maria's parents too were only a short walk away. We must have been smothered to death. No wonder I went off to university as soon as I did. Maria didn't escape for another year, and then she came to join me in Guelph.

The thought of those early days still rankled her. "We never really had any freedom to do what we wanted in those days. I felt a lot of resentment, I guess, about that." She was understating the case and, as usual, being her old tentative self about the nightmare she'd had to endure. "There was a big blowup between your mom and mine."

"What was that about?"

"It had something to do with Ana. They were both so possessive."

The whole ugly incident came back to me in a rush. As a student, I had no income except my student loan, and Maria, because of the baby, had not found a job. So she and our daughter had to shack up with her parents. I stayed with them on weekends, the three of us crowded into what had once been Maria's room. Ana was crying a lot at night—no more than any other child, but she was doing a good job of keeping us awake. I never did well without my sleep, especially when I was under pressure from being a penniless student in my first year at university. I lost my cool one night at about three in the morning. Maria had for the umpteenth time jumped up to tend to Ana. I, in a fit of anger, yelled from my bed at my daughter, in what I thought was a whisper, words that were so harsh I can no longer say them.

When I think of this now, I'm ashamed and embarrassed. It seems like absolute madness, but my choice of words had no significance beyond the release of frustration. I was crazy about my daughter, but at the ripe old age of twenty, I was also a bit crazy period, especially without sleep and living in the cramped quarters of Maria's tiny bedroom in my new in-laws' house while trying to do schoolwork. Maria's mother, who slept in the bedroom right next door, heard me and was not given to the subtleties I use now to rationalize it.

"Did you call your mom the day she came rushing up to the front door?" Maria asked.

"No. I remember it like this. When your mother confronted me about my 'nasty little outburst' the next day, she told me not to call her grandchild the terrible name I had called her. Looking back on it now, I can understand her position entirely. She thought, I suppose, that I didn't care about Ana, that I was ashamed of her, and that I wanted to disown her. All of this was rubbish, of course; I'd actually forgotten about the whole incident by the time I got home from school. But I was pissed off about her interfering in our business. So she and I got into an argument, and she told me to get out. Next thing I knew, she was on the phone to my mother, telling her to come and get me or she'd call the cops. This was not the thing to say to Maggie Glascoe about her son."

Maria was chuckling at the soap opera that she was trying hard to remember. "What happened next?"

"We were sitting on the doorstep outside, when my mother came running up to the door, white as a sheet and out of breath. I thought she was going to have a heart attack. She'd run the entire way from her house to yours and was in warrior mode. I asked her, 'What the hell are you doing?' and jumped up to grab her. 'That bitch isn't going to call the cops on you!' she said. Then she banged on the front door, and your mom, incredibly, opened the door and let us in—I guess because she didn't want a scene on her doorstep. They had a terrible row inside, and I had to hold my mother back from hitting yours. She was equally angry but visibly frightened. She clearly hadn't banked on this kind of madness. Neither had I. It all seemed so over the top."

The battle of the titan mothers made Maria and me laugh now. It fit so well into that category of absolutely nutty conflicts that come about from next to nothing.

"The strange thing is," I added, "your mother and I eventually became the best of good friends again. She was good to me."

"She was very fond of you, and so was my dad."

"How about my parents and you?"

"Your dad was fine. I got along well, very well, with him. Your mom and I got along too, but not really."

This was the tentative Maria speaking again. I waited for some details.

"It was superficial. I don't know why I have so much resentment about her. I don't know where it all started. She was basically good to me. I don't remember much," Maria said sadly, "ever since that stroke."

She'd had the stroke in her forties. Nobody seemed to know the cause; she wasn't a smoker or a drinker. There appeared to be no serious damage after the initial recovery period, except that she seemed to have trouble with her long-term memory. I wasn't totally convinced: forgetting is as important as remembering. It had been a long, long time ago, and maybe it was too much to ask of anyone to remember details from this period. But the pain that Maria and I had experienced over our breakup and even before this, over the buffoonery of our desperate parents, was colossal. Perhaps she had long ago blocked things out because they were too painful to remember.

"Maybe the resentment was related to Ana, since your mom was so possessive. Maybe it was the way she was with you. You were always right."

Me again. Why didn't I ask Maria to expand on this? She was finally coming to some kind of point. Maybe I was the one who wanted to forget now. Maybe I didn't want to hear the truth about what our relationship was really like or how the unhealthy intimacy between my mother and me affected it. But Maria was clearly uncomfortable with this line of conversation, and I didn't want to push her.

Instead, I asked her what she remembered about all the places we'd lived in later in our nomadic student life—she had eventually enrolled in the university along with me. I wanted to hear her memories of Guelph, Elora, Ottawa—but she remembered almost nothing.

"Your parents came to visit us in Ottawa. So did mine. I hated that city so much; I was glad when anyone came to visit. I remember us driving from Ottawa a lot to visit them at the Lido. She made the best steak pies. We had some great dinners at the Lido."

Dinners at the Lido—it sounded like something out of *Casablanca*, when in fact, it was a painfully mundane experience for both Maria and me. I was more convinced than ever that she genuinely couldn't remember all the poison because she had buried it long ago.

"Maria," I said, "the relationship between you and my mom was twisted."

"Yes, but I don't know why or how it all got started. I know I got along really well with your dad. Your mom, at best, put up with me. She had a nice way of saying some really nasty things. After you and I'd split up, you became sick with food poisoning. I think you, young Bobbie, and Ana came to have Dad's spaghetti. Your mother later told my mom that Dad's pasta made you sick."

"That wasn't true," I reassured her. "Everyone else who ate it was fine. We all went to an Italian festival at the park afterwards. But later in the day, I had a bite or two of pizza from a stall in the park that made me ill. It must have been tainted."

"Maybe I was too young when I knew her," Maria added apologetically. "Too young to realize what she was doing and saying."

Maria and I were divorced in the early '70s. She was out of touch with my parents for a long time after this and had almost no contact with my mother until she came to my dad's funeral.

"My mom wanted to come to the service," Maria recalled. "She really liked your dad. But I expected Eddie and Jill to pick her up, and they apparently thought I was picking her up. So there we all were, at the funeral, before we realized nobody had picked Mom up. She was very upset about that."

Jill was Maria's sister, and Eddie was Jill's husband. I was amazed and grateful that they had come to the funeral. I'd arranged for the service purely for my mother. A Presbyterian minister mouthed a few banalities, and my mother wept all through the ceremony. My father's half brother, Johnny, from New York, was there, and my mother's sister, Betty, and her husband, Pat, came in from Saskatchewan. Surprisingly, a number of friends from the apartment building my parents lived in showed up.

"At the reception," Maria said, "your mom seemed to stay in the bedroom most of the time. When she did come out, I remember her saying, 'What am I going to do? What's going to happen to me?' She seemed to be concerned only about herself. She never mentioned your dad. It was all me, me, me."

"I don't know if you remember the incredible faux pas she made at that reception. I don't even know if it can be classified as that, because she never expressed regret at having made it. The only friends who showed up to the reception outside of family were two old friends from Glasgow, a bit younger than Mom and Dad. They had been close to my parents for a while but were soon turned off by what the drink did to my father and what my mother was like without any drink at all. Dad tended to become crude and incoherent, while Mom was just batty all the time. And when their guard was down, their interaction was something close to theatre of the grotesque. The friends just didn't hang around after a while. But they dutifully came to the funeral. They were the first to leave. Mom tried to persuade them to stay, but they insisted that a daughter-in-law was coming over that day. As soon as she said this, I cringed because I knew Mom was about to stick her foot in her mouth."

"What did she say?" Maria chuckled.

"With her two current daughters-in-law sitting in the room listening and her former daughter-in-law sitting right beside her, she said, 'Och, ye don't have to bother wi' hur!' The way she accentuated the pronoun made her contempt and its target crystal clear. My mother, as you said, only cared about her own immediate family, and daughters-in-law just didn't cut it. That was a very ugly moment. Really embarrassing. I escaped into the bathroom, I think."

There was perhaps no more fitting way to end this conversation. Maria had not told her own story, the story of her own pain and resentment and what it all came from. I was the one doing the reminiscing.

We uttered a few final niceties and bid each other goodbye.

9
The Hoist

I step out of the elevator, and a group of patients congregates in the lounge. Some are chatting; some are just watching in silence. A man fully dressed in shirt, pants, and outdoor shoes sits in a wheelchair in the middle of the curving hallway, staring unflinchingly at the elevator, waiting for an unknown visitor. Another man's voice echoes across the floor periodically like the howl of a wounded animal.

When I reach my mother's room, three of the four beds are empty. Only Mrs. Mohammed is lying down today, behind the privacy screen and surrounded by attendants who are, I suppose, washing her down. My mother, surprisingly, looks at first as if she's relaxing in a deck chair by the window. In reality, she is slouched uncomfortably in a wheelchair with her legs raised on an elaborate footrest. Her eyes are tightly closed, and her forehead is wrinkled. I pull her head back to centre it on the cushioned back of the chair so that it doesn't slip off. She wakes up, rolls her eyes, and fixes her gaze on me. Her eyebrows come alive, and her lips begin to move as if she wants to speak.

"So you want to have a chat today, do you?"

She lifts her leg as if making a supreme effort.

"Or maybe you want to get up. Is that it?"

I beam into her face, congratulating myself on having elicited such a strong response, until I realize everything here has been reduced to nothing more than the basics of biological functioning. She is concentrating all her efforts on trying to fart.

"Hi there," says a nurse who has been involved in a flurry of activity around Mrs. Mohammed. "I'm Connie, and I'm looking after her now."

"Good," I say with a sense of relief that somebody is.

"She's on antibiotics."

"Again?" I say with some surprise. "For what?"

"For his bedsores."

A Filipino-Canadian, she catches me off guard with her occasional confusion of personal pronouns. I have a sudden flash that my mother is in fact someone else, a complete stranger—not my mother at all, which isn't so far off the mark.

The nurse pulls up the sheet that is draped over my mother to show me what she's talking about. I can't really see what I'm supposed to be looking at, because the sores have been expertly patched up.

"He has sores here and there," she says, pointing to the patches. "They were getting worse. Going right inside."

I recoil in discomfort.

"So we had to put her on antibiotics to stop the infection." Connie had located the right pronoun. "Now he's getting better. Looks good today."

"I suppose," I said under my breath.

Everything is relative. My mother's feet look to me like those of a corpse. Their skin has the texture of dried fish scales, and her toenails are blue. I thank the nurse for her efforts, but I shiver internally at what she is up against.

The nurse leaves and comes back moments later with a wheeled contraption, something that looks like it came from some kind of strange fitness center where people torture themselves in the name of exercise. I sit down some distance away from what promises to be a spectacle.

After manoeuvring my mother's wheelchair out into the middle of the room, Connie and a colleague who has been attending Mrs. Mohammed then pull out some hidden straps attached to the reinforced sheet my mother has been lying on, transforming it into a large makeshift bag. They hook these up to the contraption, which slowly takes on the form of a hoist. Then they raise her slowly until she is suspended like a trapped animal, her head limply dangling over the side of the bag. The top sheet falls away to reveal my mother's legs hanging from a giant diaper, legs that look for all the world like the drumstick limbs of a Holocaust victim. The skin around her thighs is as unblemished as a baby's, but it lies so slack across her knee joints that it could be used to demonstrate a lesson in anatomical bone structure and has loosened so much that it has gathered into numerous folds like a pair of old socks around her ankles.

My mother sleeps all through this, but I'm anxious they might drop her.

"That wouldn't be such a bad thing," whispers the madman, suddenly sneaking up behind me. I can't see him today, but I can feel the heat of his red face creased by the wrinkles of a mean spirit and frustrated discontent.

"What are you doing here?" I ask without moving my lips, for fear that the hospital staff will think I've gone with my mother and keep me there.

"Look at her, man," he hisses. "She doesn't know where she is. If they dropped her now, she wouldn't know what hit her. She'd be better off. Just look at those bedsores. Think of the antibiotics. How much more can she stand? Tell me you don't agree."

I say nothing and anxiously watch the nurses guiding my mother toward the bed. They lower her, carefully pulling her legs out from under her body and positioning her head on the pillow. She resumes her customary fetal position. Everything's back to normal. The madman has gone as quickly as he arrived.

"Hi, Dora," Connie says to Mrs. Garceau, the lady from the adjacent bed, who suddenly appears in the doorway after one of her many tours of the hallways. Dora does not reply, and the nurses leave. She sits down on her bed, staring intently at me while she chews a cookie, her lips flapping like those of a lapdog trying to swallow a bone. I smile and say hello. She grins like a robot, finishes her cookie, lies down, and falls asleep in a matter of seconds.

I get up to have another word with my mother before I go. She's asleep too, worn out, no doubt by her high-flying antics from a few minutes ago. I wake her up. Her pale blue eyes fix on mine until I move out of her line of vision. Like the eyes of a newborn infant, they seem unable to follow movement.

"It's all so strange, Ma," I whisper to her. "All of this."

I'm baffled by my own emotions, new ones that keep arising at each encounter with the gradually retreating familiarity of my mother. Bafflement always serves as an invitation to the pontiff of my soul, the master of my heart, the eternally benign Zen monk, to make a solicitous appearance.

He pops his head in the door and toddles into the room of my mind like one of the patients.

"So," I say provocatively.

"So?" he replies with undisturbed equanimity.

"Is it the horror of the degradation of the flesh that's bothering me now?"

"No," he says with his usual maddening self-assurance. "Not exactly."

"Is it the shock at the disgraceful meanness of life?"

"Maybe."

I feel the need to sit down. I slip into the wheelchair left by my mother's bedside, feeling like a client taking his position on the therapist's couch. The Zen monk glances at my mother and then at me. He speaks compassionately but wholly without sentimentality.

"It's the *enormity*"—he stresses the word with a gesture—"of the suffering. The suffering in the deep, painful furrows on her face, in the wound of her toothless mouth, in the grotesque contortions of her body, in the bones stripped of all flesh. The enormity of all this while the world just outside the window, as you have already noticed, carries on obliviously in its own silly, stupid way—toward what? It's the effrontery of death making its strategic appearance in the life of a loved one. Nothing more. Nothing less."

A white-haired man, Victor, wearing a seedy woolen shirt over garish red-and-blue pyjamas, strides into the room and makes a beeline for me, as if I were the oasis in his desert. He moves his lips, but nothing comes out.

"I can't hear you," I tell him, raising my hand to my ear.

"Are they having a party here?" he asks in his loudest voice, a feeble whisper that is almost lost in the surrounding racket of hospital noise.

"Yes," I reply. "I think that's what you could call it."

He nods in satisfaction, turns, and shuffles back the way he came.

The Zen monk looks at me and smiles.

"I think," I say to him, "it's time to go."

10
Spiderweb

Wwhen she could still speak, my mother once told me about a dream she had. She recalled only part of it, where she was hanging by a thread secured by some invisible fixture in the sky like the first filament of a spider's web suspended from the ceiling. She had no idea how she came to be there or what she was about to do, but she knew with a knowledge that seemed to be deeper than the dream that if she let go of the thread, she would instantly cease to exist.

When I flew to Houston to meet my brother, Robert, and hear his story, as I told him in an extended conversation about our family, I wondered how much of the family spiderweb he might be able to untangle. In the past twenty years, we had been in touch occasionally, mainly through our parents, but this was the first time I had visited him on his home territory in the USA. Ours was not what you would call the most brotherly kind of relationship.

Robert's name was never shortened within the family, because my mother's working-class pretensions would never allow it. While I had become the apple of my mother's eye in later years, when Robert had more or less flown the coop, throughout my childhood and beyond, it had always been made clear to me that he was a cut above everybody else, including me. Robert was nine years older than I was. Apart from the few occasions when we were both at home as children, we saw little of each other. He was deeply alienated from both our mother and father, for different reasons, and lived much of his childhood and youth with his grandmother. When he was eighteen, then the legal age for just about everything in Scotland, he decided to emigrate to Canada. On the day he received a letter of conscription from the Royal Air Force, he left for Greenock to catch the ocean liner to Montreal. From that day on, my brother was a veritable stranger in my life.

I have little recollection of Houston, except for the miles of concrete from the airport to the city, because we stopped at Robert's rather glum grey stucco-sided suburban house only for a change of clothing and then left. His wife, Elaine, was away in England visiting family, a trip that had been planned to coincide with mine, since she could barely stand the sight of me—or the other members of our family, for that matter—something I hoped Robert might talk about, though I was more than a little apprehensive about raising the issue. In any event, he and I headed out on the five-hour drive to Corpus Christi, where he owned a condominium with a dock for his boat, the current passion of his life.

The trip to Corpus Christi was painful in more ways than one. I had always known a handsome man with a quiet charm, quick wit, and mischievous sense of humor, someone who by his stature always seemed taller than he really was (an inch above me) and who had never endured a day's illness in his life—as far as I knew. But now sitting beside me was someone whose frame had been weighed down by time and whose striking blond hair had turned not grey but an oily, rusty brown, perhaps due in part to his recent poor health. He was suffering from a persistent, extreme pins-and-needles sensation all the way down one side of his body, a condition that none of the many specialists who examined him could diagnose. It was impossible for him to either sit or stand comfortably. I offered to take the wheel, but he insisted that it was better to drive and be distracted than not to drive and to endure the discomfort. This not only was painful for me to watch but also interfered with his ability to concentrate on the small talk to pass the time in the car. So I looked out the window a lot and tried to distract him with my observations of the passing landscape.

What I saw was almost as painful to me as my brother's plight: the reality of the Texas countryside—at least as it is between Houston and Corpus Christi. It was like landing on the moon. Every few miles, an oil refinery loomed up on the horizon. Not just an ordinary oil refinery of the kind I had known in my limited Canadian experience, but an extraordinary one—huge, massive, sprawling—a blight on the landscape. Along this five-hour stretch of highway, I counted more than the sum total of all the refineries I had ever seen in my life—dozens of monster factories paying homage to the oil gods, each one spewing out a cloud of grey misery into the air. I couldn't help but wonder about the timing of my brother's illness, since it coincided with his arrival here. But I was not about to launch into one of my environmentalist tirades to a man who had devoted his life to the technological idols of his time.

Robert had significant intellectual gifts and talents. He was probably a mathematical genius and certainly a gifted aeronautical-design engineer. My brother had just recently taken early retirement from the Canadian Space Agency, where he had been chief engineer in charge of research and development. He had quit in anger because the federal government had decided to move the agency to Quebec for its own spurious political reasons. He was not going to be railroaded at this late period in his life into learning French. After a brief, unsuccessful stint as a self-employed aeronautics consultant, he took a job at the Johnson Space Center, where he was able to fulfil his lifelong dream of working, at least indirectly, with NASA.

I was relieved when, in the distance, I could see the skyline of our destination, though my relief gradually turned to something close to horror. What I had taken to be a large, modern city was indeed Corpus Christi, but it was in fact a relatively small town, literally wedded to a gigantic oil refinery. The two were constructed side by side and looked for all the world like a single strange unit of not-quite-human urban landscape. This was where I spent the next few days with no escape. Even on the beach, where I walked with my brother every day in his effort to find some kind of relief from his discomfort, we were never out of sight of this screwy configuration, what I could only think of as "architechnology."

I was here to talk, however, so I stuck to my agenda and tried to close my eyes to everything else. Robert's condo, fortunately, faced a man-made waterway, where his boat was nestled in its own dock. To begin our long-awaited conversation about family, we sat out on the balcony overlooking the waterway, beyond which, just out of eyesight, lay the open water of the Gulf of Mexico.

I've often been struck by how little we know about our own families. Historians and scholars never tire of documenting the lives of the powerful and wealthy, yet most of them, if they are anything like me, know next to nothing about their own families' histories. Even when we think we know something, it often doesn't amount to much or is quite wrong. The fuzziness of our recollections never seems to get resolved. Family myths are a fact of human life. I was gradually discovering the real meaning of these thoughts in the case of my own family.

My brother started his story by telling me where he was born, which, to my surprise, was not where I'd thought he was born.

"I was born in Motherwell Hospital. You were born there too," he said. I quickly corrected him.

"I was born at home, 62 Omoa Road Cleland, the same place as Dad."

"God, I didn't know that."

What else didn't we know about each other? A great deal, as it turned out.

"One of the earliest memories I have, going back to early infancy, is about Dad," Robert said with an impish little-boy smile. "I remember, in a disembodied way, sitting on his knee, him rolling the loose tobacco from the old Woodbine packets into cigarette paper to make up a smoke." Then the smile faded. "Other than that, I don't have any early recollection of Dad."

Our dad, Bob Glascoe, was the son of a lifelong miner. After leaving school at fourteen, he'd spent his early years "down the pit" before joining the army—the Black Watch—sometime in the 1930s. With his shiny black hair, which he wore combed back from his forehead; his dark eyes; and his brooding manner, Bob cut a good-looking figure in his army uniform. He was not a well-educated man, but he had a rough-hewn intelligence with a good dose of ambition combined with the spirit of adventure. He wanted to be a career soldier at a time when it still meant something, at least in conventional terms. It took me many years to realize the curious irony that my father had been a member of the British colonial force sent to India to prop up the crumbling British Empire, a force commissioned to quell the homegrown uprising led by one of my great mentors, Mahatma Gandhi.

Bob's aspirations were squashed halfway through this mission, when his father was hurt in a mine accident. His family—the injured father, his sister, a stepmother, two stepsisters, and a stepbrother—needed his help as a breadwinner. My father's commanding officer, curiously, gave him the option of staying with the regiment or returning home. For my father, there was no question of what he had to do, although it was a bitter decision, because it meant not only returning to the oppressive depths of the Scottish pits but also supporting a family that, to him, was mostly alien.

My brother was born in 1938, a year or so before the beginning of World War Two. When our father was conscripted into the army this time, he disappeared from his first son's life for the next six years. With the Chindits, a battalion of well-trained fighters anointed for this job by none other than Winston Churchill himself, he was parachuted in the middle of the night into the jungles of Burma, behind Japanese front lines. Their objective was to conduct guerilla warfare against the enemy and lay the groundwork for a British invasion. Dad had gotten himself into a war that involved being targeted by deadly, accurate snipers; engaging in close and sometimes hand-to-hand combat; and living in constant fear of being discovered, captured, and tortured by the surrounding Japanese forces. In the end, the great invasion never happened, and he and his mates—those who were left after the jungle warfare—had to march two hundred miles back to British-held territory, enduring yellow fever, dengue, malaria, and dysentery along the way. Many collapsed on the long march and never made it home. My father, above all, was a survivor—this fact alone merited the medals he earned for this feat.

The terrible gap this absence left in his son's early life would never be bridged, not even when he returned. Robert was raised by our mother for the early part of his life during wartime, when many of the conventions of ordinary life broke down, no less so in my family than in many others. My brother was not unhappy during this period, but his happiness was not due to his mother, whose attentions he never seemed to get enough of.

"I remember being in a big chair in the living room in our first home in Cleland, not long after I was born, although Dad wasn't around that day. I was screaming my lungs out, as I recall, because the air-raid sirens were going off."

It wasn't simply the fact that he remembered this event from so early on that was so remarkable to me, but the naive oversimplification of an almost sixty-year-old memory from infancy coupled with the clear implication of condemnation in his voice.

"Mom came running in to pick me up—what was she thinking? Why was I, a baby, left unattended in the first place?"

This was not the first time in our conversation that I'd had to bite my tongue and remember that I had asked to hear *his* story. I hadn't come here to argue with him about his interpretation of events but to hear his side of things, to find out more about who Maggie Glascoe was. Who my brother was had already begun to emerge.

"Mom and I moved to Glasgow during the war, to live with Gran and the rest of the family in the top story of the Saracen Street tenement."

Many of the Glasgow tenements, by today's standards, were unfit to live in—veritable slums—though some, such as the Saracen Street ones, where Gran's family lived, were like royal apartments in a five-storey sandstone block, with an open corridor called a "close" running through the ground floor of the building from back to front. The flats were arranged in pairs on each floor. Each one boasted its own bathroom—a feature unavailable in the older tenements—and ten-foot-high windows in every room.

"My first memory of Gran," Robert said with unalloyed glee, "is her opening the door at the top of the Saracen Street stair, crying, 'My wee boy!'"

Our gran seemed always to be the same gentle, round lady with a kindly face and a bad leg, a leg that had been broken in youth and poorly set afterward so that it had never healed. We didn't think of Gran as physically disabled; she was a profoundly cheerful spirit who kept on going no matter what obstacles were put in her way. She was an uneducated working-class woman who was sustained by her naive faith in God and a heart the size of the moon. Gran used to sing hymns at home, not for proselytizing reasons, but in the same way others might sing pop songs: for the love of it—"Joy to the world, the Lord is come!" It lightened her days as well as ours, though perhaps not for the same reasons.

And when she sang this hymn, she really meant it. She exulted in the sheer joy of singing. Gran came from another time. Born in 1892, she was our living link with the nineteenth century. Even when I was a boy in the '50s, she still wore her grey hair rolled back in a circle of curls that were wrapped in a hairnet in the old Victorian style.

"My earliest recollection of the Saracen Street flat," Robert added with a grin, "is looking out the window onto the street below, where the tramcars turned the corner." Now he was speaking like the engineer he had become. "You could see how the rooftop arm of the old 812 tram, built in 1900, with the rounded front and orange-and-green coloring, slid along the overhead wire rail curving around the turn."

It was clear enough that the war years were not an unhappy time for my brother. He was smothered in love, not so much by Mom but by Gran and the rest of the family. "Gran's house was a warm and happy place. Although Dad was long gone by now, the whole of Gran's family was there—Aunt Betty; Uncle Don; your namesake, Uncle Andrew; Mom; myself; and, of course, Gran and Granpa."

He moved from one happy memory to another like an excited child, laughing out loud at the images still vivid in his mind. "One of the many funny things that happened on Saracen Street. Somebody baked a cake and placed it on the windowsill to cool. I got up there—must have been three or four—and *accidentally* pushed it off. It landed on the lady's fish down below!"

Next was the first of many cat stories. "We had one cat after another. They were all black and all called Ranger because Uncle Andrew was such a fanatic football fan. Mom tormented the life out of the cat. One day, she tormented it to distraction. It leaped up onto the pulley, which was quite high up in the kitchen. She went after it still, and in its desperation to escape, it turned and blindly leaped out the top of the open window." He was laughing so much that he could hardly continue the tale. "It fell the full five stories. Mom was horrified because she actually loved the cat! It was her primary source of home entertainment. She ran out the door and down the stairs. Meanwhile, the cat bolted past her on its way up the stairs before she was halfway down. It flew into the flat in a fury, as if it had just seen a ghost!

"Do you remember the sideboard?" he said, suddenly turning to something else that this memory prompted.

"Gran's old sideboard?"

"Yes, she had that from Saracen Street."

The sideboard he was referring to was one that should have been treated as a family heirloom, but in our household, nothing was treasured beyond its usefulness. It was a worn but still-stately item of Old World dining-room elegance, featuring twin cabinets and an oval mirror set in a decorative hand-carved bail and rosettes frame, with cabriole legs and bracket feet, and finished with a rich russet French-polish sheen. Gran must have inherited this from her mother when she got married. She would never have had any money to buy it. To her grandchildren, the sideboard was a treasure chest of her personal history, a family shrine where all her working-class mementoes found their final resting place.

"I used to climb inside that cabinet," Robert said with the giggle of an urchin. "I remember this because my hair would get caught in the glue in the corners, and I couldn't move without pulling it out."

My brother clearly cherished the childhood memory of the Saracen Street flat, which had multiple and spacious rooms, a fireplace in each one, high ceilings, unfinished wooden floors, and light streaming in through big windows. Above the landing, outside the door, there was even a skylight that, on sunny days, bathed the varnished oak door in a kingly radiance and cast the stairwell in palatial grandeur—at lease it appeared so to a little boy from the country.

"In those early days, I could get into and under a lot of things," Robert said with a laugh. "One time, when the sun was streaming in those big windows of the living room, Aunt Kitty and some other relatives of Gran were visiting from England. These three lovely ladies, probably in their early forties, were sitting at the table, playing cards with Gran. I crawled under the table without being noticed and found myself gaping at four pairs of ladies' drawers. I remember Aunt Kitty's in particular. They were immaculately white with big blue polka dots. I don't know why I remember this so many years later. I was too young to have any interest in this. It was just such a wonderful image. Maybe because Aunt Kitty was such a warm person. She doted over me."

Kitty Thornton was Gran's sister who lived in Kent. The only long trips I ever knew Gran to take were those she embarked on to see Kitty. Robert travelled with her several times, as he recalls, without Mom—and during the war years, to boot. Given the overprotectiveness my mother would later develop, this seemed rather strange, and I said so to Robert.

"I suppose," he said, "but the war never prevented us from travelling to Kent or London. One time, I was taken out in the middle of the night, the sirens howling, to the bomb shelter during the Blitz. We could hear the raid, airplanes buzzing overhead, and bombs exploding around us. The Thornton house was damaged that night, although luckily, as it turned out, the bomb was a dud. My recollection is that it went right through the bed, the one I would have been sleeping in, without exploding. I would have been killed in any event. I think that was the closest we ever came to being directly hit."

"I remember the bombing in Glasgow too," he continued. "We would point to the planes being picked out by the floodlights as we ran to the shelters, and we could hear the guns going off and see the flak crackling around the targets. The Germans destroyed Clydebank and the shipbuilding docks. We took a tram ride through the wreckage one day. Everything was reduced to rubble on either side of the tracks. Lots of folk killed down there. The shelters behind our tenement were built out of brick, with flat foot-thick cement roofs. The bombs would presumably blow themselves out on this rooftop, though I don't remember that theory ever being tested by my experience."

"Where was Mom in all of this?" I asked

"She was working at Mains'."

"The munitions factory on Hawthorn Street?"

"I don't know if they made weapons," Robert said. "It was a steel factory. She was there through the war years, operating a crane up and down tracks that ran along the ceiling."

"You've just unlocked one of my memories from childhood," I said, "of a story about Mom being widely respected as a highly skilled worker, somebody that her male factory colleagues had to reckon with. Do you know about this?"

"I don't. I just remember that I had to be in the house by the time she got home from work. One time, she caught me outside after she had clocked off, and dragged me upstairs. Gran opened the door and scolded her: 'The we'an has to get oot sometime, Maggie!'"

"What did Mom say?"

"Oh, I don't remember anything she said. She probably took no notice at all."

"Maybe it was the bombing incident in Kent that led to all this," I said.

"Maybe," he replied without conviction. "I didn't see her much during the week. But I remember one time, she was dancing with a man I'd never seen before, in the hallway of the Saracen Street flat. I just remember Mom looking up at him amorously as he pushed her against the wall with his body. I grabbed hold of his leg and screamed. That's as much as I recall. What can you make of that?"

I knew what I could make of it, but I wanted to hear his explanation. It never came.

Robert's mood was beginning to shift as his remembered self grew older and some of the more troubling memories bubbled up from this part of his life. He began to show me the scars on his body, the marks of time that served as records of his pain. The scars were a vivid demonstration that his remembrance was not an abstract recollection of a past that was dead and gone but a reactivation of what had come before—the living recrudescence of wounds that continued to inflict pain in the language of blood, here visibly inscribed on his body.

One of these wounds involved Uncle Don, my mother's twin. The year was 1942. Robert was about four at the time, which would mean that Don was twenty-two. It was one of those curiously strange moments that revealed so much of the character of Granny's oldest son, a man whose role in the puzzle of the family history would turn out to be pivotal, as I would only find out later from his sister, my aunt Betty.

"Uncle Don was sitting at the fire." Robert's voice was becoming raspy as if he had a lump in his throat. "He was leaning forward in the easy chair, holding a chain over the flame. I stood there beside him, watching what he was doing. Then he eased the chain away from the heat, turned to look at me, and motioned for me to grab the chain. He didn't say anything, not a word. Not thinking, I grabbed the chain. I don't know if I still have the scar. See that?" he said, lifting up his left hand for me to see. "That's the cut I got with the spade, but that there's the chain burn."

The mark was still clearly visible. I suddenly remembered that this was the same Uncle Don who brought me to tears in an incident that took place years later. He was a handsome but stocky man with a tough demeanor, a bricklayer with rough, chiseled hands, a small-time gambler who liked to dress in suits when he wasn't at work. He could be charming and seductive, rough and reckless, mean, cruel, and sadistic.

I remember the day it happened. I was playing football with the other kids on a Glasgow street, when Uncle Don appeared. Smiling at me and waving, he called me over. "Andy, could you come here a wee minute, son?" I was happy to see him and quickly ran over to say hello. His smile abruptly disappeared, and with the blank, unflagging gaze of an executioner, he slapped me, a boy of eight or nine years, heavily across the face, knocking me sideways. I had taken a candy apple that I apparently wasn't entitled to. It had been the result of a misunderstanding, but I never got the chance to explain. Don wasn't given to such subtleties. I could feel the stinging heat of that slap now as my brother recounted his story.

"I never thought much about this for a long time," Robert continued.

"Maybe you should have," I said rather bluntly. I wanted to hear more about Don, but my brother was not as inclined as I was to get to the bottom of our family's story or the hazy childhood memories that troubled me. This story was almost as frustrating for me as the cryptic story of the half cup of tea he was about to tell me—a story that would remain thoroughly unexplained until I later spoke with aunt Betty.

"Something else happened at Saracen Street that stands out in my mind," he tentatively began. "It isn't relevant to anything, really; it was a mystery that never got solved. Gran and I came home one day; everybody else was at work. A half-finished cup of tea sat on the bedside table in the middle room, Gran's room. We first thought that Don had been in for some reason. He had a fiancée or was married at that time—don't remember which."

"So what was the outcome?" I asked.

"I can't tell you anything more about it. I don't know."

So why tell me anything? I wondered. Robert just shrugged and shook his head. I couldn't figure out whether he was naive about the shenanigans in Granny's family or too prudish to speak of them. Either way, I never heard much about them from him. Notwithstanding Uncle Don's cruelty, Robert seemed to remember the Glasgow days with genuine happiness. Perhaps because of this, because he was babied and overprotected by most of the family around him, he wanted to keep those memories intact.

With his father in exotic lands halfway across the world and his mother working long hours five and a half days a week, it is hardly surprising that Robert forged a strong bond with Gran. She loved him to death and spoiled him, not with material things—nobody had any money to spare—but with a fondness that knew no bounds. He, in turn, was more attached to her than to his mother. The depth of their love can be measured by another scar he showed me on his chest, the one left from a traumatic tea burn.

"You know how Scots are with their tea. It has to be made with the water literally boiling out of the kettle spout. So that it's strong. Not like the tepid stuff over here. One time, Gran was making a cup of tea. As she came out of the kitchen, teacup and saucer in her hand, I was running down the hall, calling out her name, and I crashed right into the hot cup of tea, which splashed all over my chest. *The pain!* Excruciating. It's still sensitive to this day.

"Gran was traumatized as much as I was by the tea burn. Next thing I knew, I was in the doctor's office just down the street. But no one there seemed to have any sense that this was an emergency at all! Gran pleaded for help but to no avail. 'Ye'll jist have to wait yer turn, missus,' they said. And so we did, with me crying for what seemed like hours. Finally, we got in to see the doctor, a lady, but this turned into farce. She literally didn't know what she was doing."

"There must have been precious few women doctors around then. Maybe she was some kind of nurse rather than a doctor."

"I'm not so sure. We all called her a doctor. She never examined me; she just stuck iodine patches on the burn with cotton wool! Every time I went back to see her—every day, for the first while—she just ripped them off and put on some more. It was sheer agony for this five-year-old child. I don't remember Mom being there on the first visit, but it was she who later saw what I was going through and who took me to our old Cleland doctor, Dr. Cartwright. Right away, he applied an ointment that brought instant relief. And when he redressed the wound, there was no more ripping and tearing."

Our mother had become a kind of surrogate father, it seems— breadwinner, pillar of authority, and demigoddess in emergencies. Whenever I asked Robert what she said, he could not remember a single word. She was a woman without a voice in this son's life. Gran had taken over the role of nurturer in whom the milk of human kindness overflowed.

"The Saracen Street days ended with a fanfare. Mom received word that Dad was coming home. She put up Welcome Home signs, colored streamers, and balloons out on the landing under the skylight. It was like Christmas, all red and blue and yellow. I remember Dad finally coming up the stairs, this stranger who ruffled my hair and picked me up. The same day, Mom sent me on an errand. I must have been seven, going on eight, and I wanted to show Dad that I could run for a bottle of milk. But as I closed the flat door behind me, I tripped at the top of the stairs and fell all the way down the steps to the landing, clutching the bottle to my chest with one hand and the money in the other. Thank God the bottle didn't break; it would have cut me to pieces. Anyway, I just got up, dusted myself off, and ran to the shop. I sure as hell wasn't going to tell anyone I had just fallen down the stairs on the way for a bottle of milk. I distinctly remember that I wanted to show him—*him*, that man, my new father—that I could do things like this without falling and crying.

"After I came back, he let me shoot his rifle. A huge flame came out, though it was just a blank. You could do things like that in those days and get away with it! He gave me his watch—a gold pocket watch he picked up in India, complete with ornate engraving. By this time, I had dismantled all Gran's clocks to see how they worked, so I took this watch off into a corner to look inside."

I knew this watch and all the other things that came from India that day. They were the insignias of that faraway place that had become such an integral part of my childhood from the beginning: Dad's garrison cap, the rough woolen army blankets, his Star of Burma and other medals, the little steel replica of the Taj Mahal, the cushion cover with "Mother" embroidered on the front, which he brought for Gran. His own mother had died in a train accident when he was three years old, so he was grateful to Gran for treating him like one of her own sons.

"There wasn't much time for Dad to sit around. Pay for the demobbed was next to nothing. So we moved out of Saracen Street and back to Cleland."

Robert had stopped laughing and smiling for some time now. He turned in his seat, trying to relieve the pain of his ailment.

"Maybe we should stop for a while," I said.

"I don't know where it all started with Dad," Robert muttered as he rose from his chair. "It" was the profound disaffection that eventually set in between them. "I didn't turn out to be the son he expected, I guess. He never spoke more than two words to me from this time on until I was eighteen."

"Why don't we go for a walk on the beach?"

He nodded. The sky was clear, the wind brisk. The crashing of the gulf waves on the Texas coast would distract us.

11

Crowd of Pilgrims

own the hallway again, back into the whirlpool. It's packed today, with a crowd of pilgrims going nowhere. The man in the diaper is there, as is the lady in a flowery Victorian frock who seems perpetually to wait by the elevator to greet newcomers with her customary refrain: "Hello, how are you today?" The wheelchair group is lined up like an oddball phalanx around the curved window. They're at the back of the lounge, facing the elevator in wide-eyed anticipation at arriving visitors. A nurse distributing medication moves from one room to another while carrying on a conversation with the Chinese man who tags along behind her in his pajamas and slippers. His voice is barely audible above the usual din.

"You'll get your dinner at five o'clock," the nurse says lightheartedly like a teacher to her kindergarten child. "Yes, that's right, at five. Today. No, they'll bring it to your room. Yes, five o'clock. That's the dinner hour. No, you don't have to order. At five, as usual."

I stop at the nursing station, as I occasionally do, to check up on any changes to my mother's medication. A dark-skinned, lanky young Pakistani man wearing street clothes and Nike running shoes lopes along the hallway with a purpose. His mouth hangs open in something resembling a perpetual grin, and he repeatedly makes the sound of a stunted laugh. He sidles up to me as if to whisper a secret.

"Haw!" he says.

"Hi," I reply.

"Yaw senoheeaawee."

"Sorry," I say, a little embarrassed because I can't understand him. Is it because he just doesn't speak clearly, or is my hearing that bad?

"No, Ali," the nurse behind the desk scolds. "He doesn't."

Ali's grin disappears. He abruptly reassumes his loping gait and staggers down the hall.

"He was asking for a cigarette," the nurse explains with a smile.

"Oh, well, I don't smoke. So I wouldn't have been able to give him one anyway."

"He can smoke cigarettes downstairs, but we don't want patients plying them from visitors."

I get the information I want and head for my mother's room. Today, a young Jamaican-Canadian woman in a plaid jacket is feeding the patient across from my mother. The caregiver is so attractive that I don't notice anything else out of the ordinary.

"Just your onions now," she says as she lifts the spoon to the lady's mouth, "and some carrots."

We greet each other with a smile.

"Is she your mother?"

Does she see the relationship? Is it possible to pick out the resemblance between my mother as she is now and me? What do I look like? How far apart are we then? I hesitate to think too much about this.

"Yes," I reply, a little embarrassed.

I turn to my mother, and a flash of guilt strikes me in the chest, as if I have just somehow betrayed her. She, however, is unmoved. Her eyes are closed, as usual. I lightly touch her chin, her cheekbone, and then her nose, which is sensitive. She grimaces in annoyance.

"Aren't you going to open your eyes today?" I ask softly.

Her cheeks puff up as she breathes. Without lifting her lids, she squeezes her eyes together like someone trying to see when the sun strikes the snow.

"Almost done?" the caregiver asks her patient. "One more spoonful, darling."

My mother looks as if she is checking out the territory to see who's there before she opens her eyes. Eventually, she does open them.

"How are you today?" I cry with as big a grin as I can muster.

She looks blankly at me for a few minutes, rubs her toothless gums together, and slowly closes her eyes again.

"I guess the territory ain't interesting enough today, eh?"

I steal a glance at the action across the way and, to my surprise, see a new face in the bed. A grey-haired lady is sitting up and licking her chops after every spoonful of food. The nameplate above her bed says "Mrs. Henry."

"What happened to Mrs. Mohammed?" I ask the caregiver.

"Died," she says uncomfortably.

"My God! When?"

"Saturday."

I had seen Mrs. Mohammed on Friday, in her usual state, lying flat on her back, staring at the ceiling with a look of suspended terror. Her husband had come in for his daily visit and had nudged her firmly to get her attention. He had given her something to drink and talked to her in Hindi.

Although she used to be quite attentive and capable of sitting up to be fed by her husband when I first saw her, I tended to think of her in a perpetual semi-coma. I imagined she, like my mother, was parked in neutral with the motor still running, however labored and stuttering it might be. I hadn't paid much attention to her, because she hardly changed from one visit to the next. Now she was more noticeable by her absence.

"Dessert?" the caregiver says to Mrs. Henry. "Mm, it looks good."

I turn to take a good, hard look at my mother. She appears today to be in a state of unquiet repose, on a journey through the dark, almost-obliterated territory of her brain. I thought of Adèle's incredulity when I said that my visits amounted to bearing witness to her dying in slow motion. There's no doubt of that in my mind each time I see her. The question is, when will the clock stop?

"All finished?" the caregiver asks her patient. "Good. You've done very well."

She begins to pull the tray away.

"More," Mrs. Henry says.

"More? You'd like some more?"

She wheels the tray back into place.

"My goodness," the caregiver cries with a smile, "I didn't know you could eat so much."

Life, I guess, is taking its voracious course right in the spot where death has just occurred, probably many times before. Though Mrs. Henry can talk and looks better than my mother, she reminds me of what Mrs. Mohammed looked like when I first saw her. Perhaps this is the death ward—the ultimate waiting room, the last checkout counter before the final rite of passage. I just sit, watch, and listen to the stream of chatter.

"Coffee?"

Mrs. Henry refuses nothing.

"Well, m'dear. That's it for lunch," her caregiver says as she wheels away the tray.

The old lady yawns, coughs, and yawns once more.

"You off to sleep again?" the caregiver cries. "After such a big meal?"

Mrs. Henry closes her eyes.

"Wake up, sleeping beauty," her caregiver says, gently tugging her sleeve. "Let's talk about something."

The lady, however, is nodding off.

"All right, you go to sleep, and I'll relax now."

She sits down and picks up her book. But she's fidgety. She's supposed to improve the quality of life. She wants to do her job.

"Listen to this," she says to the dozing Henry in a loud voice. "I want to read you something this man says. Tell me what you think of it."

Mrs. Henry wakes up as the caregiver tugs at her sleeve and reads the passage—something about how marriages fall apart because of lack of communication when the partners discover that they have not been friends. Sometimes this is the result of a gap in education. If one partner holds a doctorate degree and the other hasn't even done the eighth grade, they might not understand each other and might drift apart.

"Do you believe that, dear?"

The old lady looks sleepily at her.

"Can you repeat that back to me?" the caregiver calls out.

Mrs. Henry, remarkably, does a fairly good job, though the words are all different from those in the book.

"Good! Now, is that a fact?" her caregiver asks.

"Yes, I think it's true," Henry whispers.

"Oh," the caregiver says, "I don't agree with it."

Mrs. Henry yawns again and nods off once more.

"Hey!" somebody yells down the hallway. "Hey!"

"Bernie!" cries a nurse from somewhere else.

"Hey! Hey! Hey!"

"Bernie!" cries the nurse. "Stop your shouting."

Mrs. Henry sleeps through all this and more, but her caregiver shakes her head.

"The people on this floor," she says, laughing to herself and looking in my direction. "I just can't believe them."

A nurse comes with juice and cookies for the cookie lady, Mrs. Garceau, who is not in her bed. The nurse begins to make the bed. Just as she's in the process of stripping off the sheets and pillowcases, Mrs. Garceau returns.

"I want to sleep!" she bellows in a foghorn voice.

"Wait! Wait! Wait!" cries the nurse, who is in no mood to put up with any belligerence.

Mrs. Garceau stands in her nightdress at the foot of the bed, her mouth quivering involuntarily, waiting impatiently for the nurse to finish.

"Do you want me to make the bed?"

"Yeah."

"Then don't rush me."

"Okay," she says, leaving the room to wander the halls again.

"I tell you," Mrs. Henry's caregiver says with a grin to the nurse, "this floor. I don't know how you people take it all day every day. This is some floor."

"I'm here because of the new health system," the nurse replies. "Because of the new environment."

"What do you mean?"

"I had a nice floor—the sixth floor. It's still my floor. A nice, quiet floor. Now they moved me up here as well. Gave me two floors. This one—"

"Well," says Mrs. Henry's attendant with an understanding laugh, "it's different."

"Very different. The way things were before, well, you can't compare," the nurse says with an air of complete self-assurance.

"I guess everything's changing."

"Everything," the nurse intones conclusively as she hurries out of the room.

The caregiver returns to her book. She yawns, pulls a cell phone from her purse, and dials a number.

"Evelyn? … Adrienne."

Her accent suddenly becomes thicker, and she has no concern for privacy, because she speaks loudly enough for me to hear. She has to in order to overcome the perpetual din.

"Went to school today? … You're so smart … Brilliant! … Mommy there? … Carol … Yes … Listen, I want to read you something. Listen to this."

She reads the passage she read earlier to Mrs. Henry.

"Do you agree with that? … So what you saying? … You support him then? … No … No, I don't … Education don't matter … Educated people can speak simple … Only up to a point … Two highly educated people don't guarantee anything … A degree don't help here … Some people have a degree and they're dumb … Why worry about society? … Society create too many problems … I don't see it like that … Hold on now … Just to please society? … But, well, then you wouldn't marry outside of … As long as you're happy is my view, whatever the appearances, because we worry too much about society instead of what makes us happy."

Mrs. Garceau returns, walks over to the side of her bed, and stares at it intently, as if studying its essential details.

"Pull that down!" she suddenly bawls in Adrienne's direction.

Startled, Adrienne turns and looks askance at Mrs. Garceau.

"What's happening here?" she asks.

"Pull that down!"

"Evelyn?" Adrienne says into the phone, "No, no, it's someone here— just a minute, please."

She puts down her cell phone and gets up to attend to Mrs. Garceau.

"This floor," she says with a smile in my direction. "I tell you."

The nurse who remade Mrs. Garceau's bed had inadvertently left in place the metal guard intended to keep patients from falling out of bed. Adrienne pulls it down and goes back to her cell phone. Mrs. Garceau, true to form, picks up her cookies, sits on the bed and wolfs them down, knocks back her juice, and promptly falls asleep when her head hits the pillow.

I've been looking out the window most of the time, turning around once in a while to see the comings and goings. My mother is still asleep. Adrienne finishes her phone call, exasperated that she hasn't yet found someone to agree with her in her disagreement over the passage in the book.

"Do you mind if I have a look?" I ask her.

"Oh, you heard me," she says, smiling. "Yes, this is it here."

It's a coffee-table book by a black writer. We discuss the passage. She tells me she doesn't agree with the bit about education being a barrier to a good marriage. I say that the writer is just using this as an example, that he doesn't mean that all marriages are doomed to failure because of differences in education. She is a bit relieved by this interpretation but goes on to tell me what her friend Evelyn said—that she wouldn't marry a white guy.

"I says to her, 'Why not? You're living in a white society. Why you want to limit yourself, girl?' I says."

There is twinkle in her eye and a lusty gurgle in her throat as she laughs.

"That way, you got less to pick from. A lot less! I married outside my own race," she says proudly and defiantly, her hands on her hips. "And what's wrong with that, I ask you?"

"Sounds like a great idea to me," I say, happy not to be challenging her and hesitant, for some reason, to tell her I have done the same.

"We're different, but if you love each other, what's the difference?" She's on a roll. I just nod.

"I'm happy," she cries.

"Yes," I say, "you look like you are."

"I don't care what society says. I'm happy."

She's been walking around the room, gesticulating with emphasis. She picks up her purse with the air of someone who's just proven a point and accomplished something.

"Well, I have to get something to eat. If I see you," she says to me as she leaves, "I see you. Nice talking."

Victor, in a brightly colored sweater and pyjama bottoms, trundles into the room. He walks right up to my chair, stands six inches from me, and looks over my head out the window. He mutters something incoherent, turns to the balcony door, and tries the handle, but it's locked. He starts to make the only empty bed in the room, but only for a few seconds. Then he gives that up for the towels by the bedside. He folds them and refolds them. Then he exits with the air of one who has successfully completed an important task.

"Time to go, Ma," I say to my unconscious mother. "You're not listening again."

I can hear the nurse in the distance, still answering the endless questions of the Chinese man who is anxious about his dinner.

"You'll get your dinner in your room … At five o'clock … Yes … That's right … Today, of course … No, no, I'm not running away … I'm going to arrange for your meal."

As I turn to leave, I see Mrs. Mohammed's name plate lying forgotten on the windowsill. On my way out of the room, I check the other name plates by the door. My mother's is still there. She still has a name. Everything's right with the world.

In a manner of speaking.

12

A House of Mirrors

I was coming to realize that the stranger I was searching for wasn't just my mother but also my father, my brother, my entire family, and, through them, myself. Only when I was able to know this family—to know its history both open and secretive, the celebrated and notorious events, its loves and its hates—could I even begin to expect to know myself, not myself as *Andy* Glascoe but myself as Andy *Glascoe*. My family, I began to realize, was who I was and what each of its members made themselves out to be. The Glascoe family had a life of its own, a life in which we all shared, from which we all developed our own way of being, whether good or bad, whether conflicted or not—a life in which this self-same family continued to live out its rich, unique, and surely peculiar destiny. It seemed to me now rather ludicrous that anyone would imagine that he or she was an isolated, atomic, self-made creature, when we were all filtered through a family sieve. I had walked into a house of mirrors. I would have to be the deity with a thousand eyes to track down anyone's identity, let alone my own.

Seeing through the eyes of my brother, Robert, I recognized that so much of what he was saying was familiar, but in the strangest way. His disaffection from the rest of us had been a part of my growing up, absorbed along the way and sitting somewhere in my mind for all these years, a frozen block of time that was an undeniable part of who I was as much as who he was. But somehow it had been forgotten because so many other things had filled up the space around it.

Robert said he didn't know where this estrangement had begun, but he did know. He had been documenting it from day one in the little Scottish village near the Lanarkshire coal mines he returned to in the late 1940s after his curiously idyllic war days in Glasgow. He had recorded it in his every judgment, every thought, every feeling, every action—in every mark on his body.

"You see that there," he said, pointing to another scar—this time on his knee—a scar I suddenly remembered seeing in my boyhood. "I got that coming from school one day behind Aitken's bakery in Cleland. I was on my hands and knees in the grass, hunting for something I dropped. Before I knew it, I had this big gash on my knee. For whatever reason, Dad was home alone when I walked in. I sat on the chair, trying to close the bleeding wound without crying. The old man never looked at it, never even said, 'You better put something on that.' He never said a word, as a matter of fact. Dad just ignored me completely. I knew then, when I was seven or eight years old, that there was something seriously wrong here. This wound—look at it—probably should have been stitched. It never got any medical attention at all, never even had a bandage on it. Somehow it didn't get infected. I don't know where Mom was, but she never did anything about it either. I remember even then, though, thinking that somebody should be doing something."

He paused to shift his weight in an effort to find some comfort from the infernal pins and needles.

"Strangely enough," he went on, "this led to a kind of self-reliance at an early age. By the time I was twelve, I'd smashed my face in a bicycle accident, chipping my teeth when I fell. A normal kid would say, 'Ma, look at this,' and she'd say, 'My God, we have to take you to the dentist.' But that never happened. I elected on my own to go to a dentist, to get some serious work done. I can't imagine any parent relying on their child now to do that."

Many thoughts were fleeting through my mind now as he spoke—thoughts about how hard it had been for my father to readjust from the war; how my mother never took care of her own teeth or either of her kids' teeth, because she was afraid of going to the dentist; and how she once told me that my father had complained about her over-protectiveness of Robert. These thoughts seemed relevant to Robert's story, but if I had uttered them, I would have sounded as if I were making excuses for inexcusable behavior. Or I might have appeared to be mocking the obvious inconsistencies in so much of his story. Perhaps I was doing both. Perhaps I was the one who didn't see my parents clearly.

Robert went on to give an account of how this inattentive father (not our mother, who "never went there") nevertheless took him "very often" to the next village to visit his Parkside granny and granpa, my father's stepmother and father. He spoke of his grandparents on this side of the family as "kind and gentle" and of their place as "a nice place to visit," in part because Dad would speak, if not to Robert, at least to Grandpa.

"There's a picture of you as a baby crawling in the grass at Grandpa's place, with Dad sitting on his hunkers beside you. I was there when that was taken."

"Were you around when I was born?"

"Of course. Dr. Cartwright arrived and tossed Dad and me out the door."

So he did know that I was born at home after all, even though he had not recalled this earlier. I silently lamented the frailty of human memory and its implications for my present quest.

"Next thing I knew," Robert added with a grin, "there was this bawling brat. From very early on, Mom sang to you. I don't know if you remember that."

I did remember. It was the earliest of all my memories, a memory deeply imprinted from infancy because it was such a terrifying experience. Mom never sang sweet lullabies to put me to sleep. She sang her own deliberately torturous version of the old Eddy Arnold song "Wagon Wheels":

Wagon wheels, wagon wheels keep on turning, wagon wheels
Roll along, sing your song, carry me over the hill.

"She would hang over your face, open her mouth up really wide, and sing, 'Waaaaaaaaah-gon wheels!' Your bottom lip would pucker out and quiver. She'd keep on singing, 'Waaaaaaaah-gon wheels,' until you were on the verge of bursting into tears."

"I've retained one or two vivid images from my infancy," I told him, "and one of them is Mom's gaping mouth and the rasping sound she made when she stretched out the words of this song. And then with a giggle, she'd pick me up and say something like 'Aw, ma wee darlin', I'm just kiddin'.'"

"Yeah, but by then, you were already howling. At the time, it seemed kind of cute, but later on, I thought it was so bloody irresponsible. She did it more than once—did it to show people your lovably funny, quivering bottom lip."

"It must have been around this time," I said, "when we were still in Cleland, that Dad, to prevent her from going dancing, one time boarded up the windows and locked her in the house when he went down the pit on the night shift. He actually nailed wooden boards across the windows so she couldn't get out. Do you know anything about that?"

"I never saw it, but I have recollections of an undercurrent in their relationship, one that welled up from the war. While Dad was away, Mom went out socially."

Robert was a master of understatement. He was also a shy man whose mother had protected him from much of the crudeness of working-class life of those days. There was something truly Victorian in his moral sensibility.

"What do you mean by that?" I asked.

"She went dancing all through the war years. I don't know how it was for a woman in that situation then, whether the physical activity of dancing was enough for her. But for a man, dancing was a means to an end."

Robert's almost Victorian reservation when it came to matters of sex was one of the peculiarities of his personality.

"And she kept on going after the war?"

"Yeah. If you take it from the male point of view, it would be abhorrent for a man to watch his wife go out dancing. I was aware that Dad didn't see Mother's virtue being intact."

"Did you hear them talking about it?"

"No. There was just something in the air. I never heard any arguments. None at all."

This would turn out to be one of the many lacunae in my brother's story. His memory was no better and no worse than anybody else's. It was just fuzzy around the edges, with a few gaping holes in the middle, into which contradictions would later insert themselves. There were also a lot of things he just didn't seem to know about. Perhaps he was too young to understand, he just wasn't present when they happened, or he blocked them all out later. Anyway, in spite of all the sadness of returning to Cleland, he spoke about this period by recalling an odd mixture of glowing and plaintive memories.

"The freedom of country living after the war, riding my bike, playing football every day, making slings and slingshot—these were the happiest years of my life."

He clearly didn't realize the cutting irony in what he had just said or in the stories of this "happiness" that were to follow. After all the years of marriage and having a family of his own, the exemplary educational achievements of a poor working-class boy, the remarkable successes of professional life—here he was, rating his poor, oppressed boyhood above all of that as the happiest time in his life. The irony even went further— the stories he told of the happy times were laced with an overriding sadness.

"We used to make everything ourselves—the sling out of a forking branch in a tree, the sling bands out of old bicycle tube, slingshot out of lead pellets. Remember that?"

"Yes," I said, "melting the lead in an old pot over a campfire and then pouring it into a clay mould. We always felt as if we were doing something really seditious."

"In a way, we were," he said. "Lead pellets in slings were dangerous, the preferred choice of weapon among poachers and gang members alike. We were neither, but you get the idea. Using these as slingshot, we would try to hit birds for fun, especially skylarks, because they used to kind of hover, almost like hummingbirds, high up in the sky."

"In today's terms, of course, it was—"

"I know—cruel. It didn't take me long to discover that on my own.

One day, when I was with Tom Baines, I actually hit a lark, and it dropped to the ground. I ran over and picked up the poor thing. Its head hung over the side of my hand, and I suddenly realized what I'd done. I tried to hide it from Tom, but he saw it. I felt so much more ashamed because he'd witnessed me doing it and, even worse, because he thought I was such a good shot. After that, I never aimed at another bird. You had to play the game of seeming to go after them—it wouldn't do to be squeamish around the other boys—but I was always a deliberately poor shot after that."

He pushed himself out of his chair to take a walk around the room and make us a cup of tea. I was glad to hear this story, in a way, because I had grown up with the image of my brother as close to perfection, someone who never did anything wrong. It was the image my mother had created of him in everyone's mind—most of all, mine. It was the reason I still called him Robert, when everyone else in the world knew him as Rob.

"Dad came out one day to play cricket with the other dads and the kids on Omoa Road."

"Came out with you? To play cricket?" I was incredulous.

"I know it's hard to believe. But the impression I had was that he was going to show me in no uncertain terms how it was played."

"What did he know about cricket?" I asked, and then it dawned on me. "He must have learned how to play from his English friends in the army."

"I guess so. Dad was no mean athlete. He'd won an award somewhere, maybe in the army again, for cross-country running."

"Once," I interjected, "when he and Mom and I were on our way home late at night from the Railway Club, where they both worked, he said to me, 'I'll race ye to the next gate.' I was about eleven or twelve then and playing soccer all the time. I beat the hell out of him, but he seemed to love it. Other than that, he never came out to play anything with me."

"The cricket game wasn't exactly what you might call natural play between father and child," Robert said disconsolately, ending the story before it had begun. "Later, when I had the misfortune of winning the egg-and-spoon race at the Cleland school gala, he made it patently clear what he thought of me. 'That's about all you could win,' he said in a way that seemed calculated to obliterate any dreams I might have of being an athlete like him. I had gangly legs and big feet, and he made me feel as if I weren't good enough for anything. And inside the house, he kept an oppressive silence and created a sense of deep unhappiness. The only time I could enjoy myself was outdoors with friends. It was the same for Mom; when you think about her situation, you can't blame her for socializing. Can you imagine going to the pictures with Dad?"

"Hardly."

"Not in a million years! I remember half a century later, here in Canada, he was drunk one night and going on about the old days. I must have said something critical. He said, 'I just wanted to reminisce.' Reminisce! It was the last thing on earth I would think of doing with him! What did I have to reminisce about? A father who never said anything to me for the first eighteen years of my life!"

Robert stood up again, grimacing with pain, either from remembrance or from the persistent pins and needles. It was hard to tell.

"Oddly enough," he continued, "Dad, although he was not an educated man, was no slouch in the brain department. When we moved a few miles away to the then-new postwar housing scheme in Newarthill—"

"The prefabs," I said, recalling the prefabricated tin houses the government had constructed for returning troops—supposedly temporary habitations that we had still been living in more than ten years after the war.

"He was secretary of the tenants' association."

"What?" I could barely believe my ears. "I never imagined he could be secretary of anything."

"I know what you mean. But Dad was intelligent. It was just so hard to draw it out of him. He had to write letters to the county council. I found one of them lying on the table. I almost fell off my seat when I read it. It was not only well written, but it made a convincing argument. I couldn't believe that Dad, the epitome of silence in my life, had written it. I was stunned."

"Talking about writing letters, do you know how he lost the three fingers on his right hand?"

"That was in Newarthill too, though he was working in the mines at Shotts. Late one night, Mom woke me up—quietly so as not to wake you. You were still quite young at the time. It was actually serious, because he was the last of a line of men coming out the pit. He had leaned against the wall of the mine and accidentally touched a bundle of detonator caps, and as he put his hand on the damn things, they exploded. Luckily, he caught the attention of the last miner out before him, and he came rushing back to help Dad out.

"Mom told me that he was in Law Hospital. I went with her to see him that night. He had a big bandage wrapped around his hand and seemed not that bad—he was sitting up in bed, talking. But there was a lot of shrapnel in his hand. He went on workers' compensation for quite a while after that. We eventually got a piano out of this"—he smirked—"and I got a bike. You must have gotten something too."

I had no recollection of any big gift from that time, and I certainly didn't get a bike. But I wanted more information about a time I couldn't recall, especially about what had happened to my father. I asked, "Did he leave the mines after this?"

"Oh yeah. I was fifteen and already working in the offices of British Rail, so my friends and I would often go to the Railwaymen's Club in Motherwell to play snooker and table tennis. I heard there that he was going to be bartender."

The Railwaymen's Club was one of those thoroughly proletarian institutions in Britain after the war, when so much of the country depended on trains. It was the working man's answer to the upper-middle-class private establishments that were designed to keep the likes of them out. The club was a sanctuary for me as a boy, when both my parents ended up working there—my father as head bartender and my mother as supervisor of the small cafeteria. With little or no parental oversight at home and my brother gone, first to Granny's and later to Canada, I ended up spending a lot of time at the club—watching TV when we still had none at home; playing darts; listening to the band at weekly dances; watching the dancers, like Mom, who was often on the floor with male and female partners alike; wandering in the lovely gardens outside and picking fresh gooseberries off the shrubs; or meandering through the golf course next door.

Most of the time, I was alone, but sometimes there were other kids like me, occasionally girls, left in the TV room at the club. I remember playing a game with a couple of them when one, a sweet and lovely blonde girl I barely knew, kissed me in a dark corner of the room. I was transfixed and, at that age, eleven or twelve, had no idea what to do in response. I don't remember following up on this at all, although I did look in the TV room in vain for the same girl many times after that. Shortly after this, perhaps to compensate, I fell head over heels for the dark-haired granddaughter of the cloakroom attendant.

The club itself started off as a beautiful old Victorian mansion, the many nooks and crannies of which I endlessly explored in delicious secrecy. I might have been looking for the madwoman in Rochester's house in *Jane Eyre*. The building lost its romantic appeal when, a few years later, they clipped on a hideous steel-sided addition.

"You didn't hear about the new job at the club from him?" I asked.

"No, he never said anything to me. It was abominable to have such a relationship. It's unnerving, even now, to think about it—the complete, ongoing silence. I mean, why?"

He remained exasperated by this perplexing mystery, even now, some forty-five years later. I could not bring myself to remind him of the war experiences that, as a child, he had not heard about but that by the time he was a youth and certainly by now, in his manhood, he should have known well. Nor could I remind him of his own recollections of Mom's "socializing," which must have been weighing heavily on the old man at that time too. Robert, incredibly, had never reflected on the impact of these things on my father. He was still viewing it all from the perspective of the hurt child. I just nodded in mock sympathy.

"Did he never talk to his friends," he continued, "to his brother, Johnny, and his two sisters, Dorothy and Mary, all of whom were always very nice to me? I know that when he went to Parkside, he had long conversations with Grandpa, but then at these times, he seemed nothing like my dad. When I look at how he could do it there and then I think about how he behaved at home, it's just incomprehensible—the horrible silence he imposed on his family for whatever reason. Later, when he came to join me in Canada, he was more conversational. But the damage was already done."

"The same thing happened to me," I said—rather gingerly because I didn't want to sound as if I were trying to minimize the suffering Robert had clearly endured on this score. "There was almost no conversation. I literally didn't know the old man until I came to Canada. I guess that move was significant for him."

My brother was writhing in his seat again. I had once or twice suggested some alternative medical practice that might help him with his condition, which none of his big-time specialists could diagnose. But he didn't want to consider them—they were "too flaky." I held back for a moment to see if he would be able to settle down or might need to take a break.

"Carry on, Andy. I'm just shifting my weight."

"Going back to the Railway Club," I said. "This wasn't long before you were to make your move to Canada."

"Dad had some trouble with the management."

As soon as he said this, I suddenly remembered the whole thing. I was astonished not only at the abrupt recollection of a forty-year-old story emerging from the cavern of my skull but also at how much of a haze I was living in. The past, so heavily covered by the mist of time, was still working itself out in the present.

Bob Glascoe, my father, had lost his mother at age three, descended into the abyss of the pit at age fourteen, and returned from the jungle of war only to slip back into the mineshaft, where he eventually lost three fingers from his right hand. He was a man whose wife seemed to be always slipping away from him and who was obviously suffering from a serious postwar depression that was never understood, let alone treated—this man had begun to find solace in drink. And being a bartender after the mine accident made alcohol easy to get. He was a man who could hold his drink, as they say, and he never lost a day of work at the Railway Club because of it. He kept the place running and, with the help of a little shot here and a little shot there, had no problem carrying on conversations at the bar with the clientele, who all had nothing short of reverence for him. They had heard about his impressive war record. I remember some drunken sod saying to me one day, "Your dad is a great man." Great or not, I never heard anything but words of praise and respect for him from his fellow workers and patrons of the Railway Club.

But the drink probably made him easy pickings for somebody, because the till was losing money. Not much—it was nothing more than a case of petty pilfering, but it was a crime. The senior manager, Mr. Heathcote, a dignified and portly man with a bald head, was one of my old man's biggest admirers. He was shocked at this discovery, although he never suspected or accused my father. I have no idea whether they ever caught the culprit, but they had to let my father go because it happened on his watch. Heathcote was crushed by this decision. My mother resigned in sympathy.

Incredibly, this momentous shift in the family's circumstances drew no further comment from Robert. It had barely affected him. He had other things on his mind.

"I myself got into a bit of trouble around this time. Did you know about that?" he asked me with some apprehension.

Once again, I felt the rush of suddenly coming to my senses, because once again, this ancient memory had been lodged somewhere in the back of my mind.

"Now that you mention it, yes, I did know something. Tell me more about it."

But Robert turned away with some embarrassment and refused to talk about it. It was something he had tucked away and had no desire to revisit. The memory, however, quietly wafted into my consciousness. He had somehow come under the influence of some lowlife in Glasgow, where he worked—an older man who had passed stolen goods on to him. I don't know what Robert's role was, but he had these goods in his possession when he was apprehended by the police. I don't know if he was charged or went to court, but I do know that he escaped conviction and ended up with no police record.

"The one thing I don't want to do here is to leave the impression that the situation between Mom and Dad had anything to do with this or that they didn't support me. In fact, for the first time in my life, I sensed something the old man felt for me, something that wasn't there before. When he was backed up against the wall, he came through."

The tears welled up in my eyes when he reminded me of the backbone and loyalty of this old man of silence. Curiously, the event reminded Robert of his own experience later with one of his sons who got caught up in some trouble and how my brother talked him through the misery, supported him, and refused to lay blame. Our old man's silent loyalty seemed to bear fruit. But this did not prevent Robert from soon drifting back into acrimonious complaint. This time, it was about how, in spite of all the painful experiences he had been speaking of, country village life meant the freedom and joy of playing uninhibitedly outside in the fields and glens of Cleland and Newarthill, an escape from the onerous confinement he had endured under Mom. Between having to work long hours at the factory and gallivanting at the dance hall during the war years in Glasgow, she felt compelled to lay down strict rules for his behaviour and kept him indoors most of the time. She was to endure much complaining about this from my father when he returned home from the war.

"Did you know that Mom and Dad were in conflict about your upbringing, that it was Dad who insisted you needed to be more independent?" I asked this provocatively because I was becoming a bit irate at Robert's continuous condemnation of our parents. True to form, he turned the point around.

"I know there was something in that," he said, his face reddening as his mood shifted, "but the background factor was that when Dad came back from the war, I was not one of the tough little nuts that could stand up to the bullies in school. The old man thought that Mom had spoiled me—fucked me up, actually."

I had heard Robert swear once or twice in my entire life, so when he did so now, I knew he was angry still after all these years. And so was I—not at them, but at him.

"I know this," he continued, "because I heard arguments on Omoa Road, arguments about my fundamental capabilities. It was well defined for me. So I knew where I stood."

The inconsistencies in my brother's stories were curious. At first, he couldn't remember arguments between our parents; now he did—especially when they related to what he clearly thought of as his own victimization.

"One day, when I was around thirteen years old, I was opening the door to escape outside, when Mom said, 'Play us a choon.' Well, as you might expect with two stubborn people, this turned into a wait-the-other-out contest. She kept me sitting on the stool by the piano for I don't know how long, urging me to play while I silently refused. When she wasn't doing this, she would hang out the window as I left, crying out to me with her rasping, teasing voice, 'Byeeeee, hansum!' God, I mean, really, it made my blood curdle. I was turning into a young man. I couldn't imagine what the neighbors thought!"

He reddened just remembering this event. "With the combination of the auld man pushing my inferiority buttons and Mom's idiotic banter, I became so shy that I couldn't speak in groups or in new situations. I just sat there like a stone. The guys I worked with in Glasgow, in my first jobs, thought I was just plain weird. But that was the legacy of Bobbie and Maggie Glascoe."

I didn't want to reinforce his hostility by telling him that I had gone through exactly the same experience, starting in my teenage years and lasting well into my twenties. When I first came to Canada, I was so mute in the presence of my new high school classmates that they thought I was gay and shunned me. I used to blush—almost purple, it seemed—when I had to speak in classes, and I would tremble and shake in the presence of girls I was attracted to. This was a horribly nullifying condition. It turned into thwarted ambition. I was afraid of the attention I would attract if I failed, even though inside, I knew full well I could succeed at anything I turned my mind to. I had been resisting my brother, but he was right in much of what he said. We had both been caught in the coiling history of our parents' suffering, and we'd been left with a painful legacy that had carried over into the rest of our lives.

We could hear birds singing outside his apartment, and his neighbors were packing up their boat for a sail. It was time for another walk to release the tension and ease Robert's maddening discomfort. Fortunately, the South Texas days were sunny and warm. Perhaps the sunshine would cheer us up.

Perhaps.

13

Red, Yellow, Blue, Green

Someone is visiting Mrs. Henry today—a tall white lady in a suit. Adrienne is sitting by her bed as a nurse attends to the patient. Mrs. Henry has a damp cloth on her forehead. Her temperature is up.

"We'll wait to see if it comes down," the nurse tells her. "If it doesn't, we'll call in the doctor. He's doing his rounds shortly anyway."

"I'm sorry for being so much trouble," Mrs. Henry says.

"That's all right," says the nurse. "Don't be sorry. It's my job."

There's less of a strain on my mother's face today. There are no red blotches on her skin.

"You know I'll always love you," I hear Henry, in a feeble voice, say to her visitor.

"I know, I know, I know," the lady replies, making an unsuccessful effort to hide her impatience.

"Are you staying awhile?"

"No, I've got to get home to do things. Lots of things to do."

My mother wakes up momentarily to fart and closes her eyes again. She hasn't noticed I'm here. I sit watching the changing expressions on her face.

Mrs. Henry's visitor is carrying on a vigorous conversation with Adrienne while the nurse is attending to Mrs. Henry. When the nurse goes, the visitor leans over to kiss Mrs. Henry, who is now sleeping with her mouth wide open, and takes her leave.

"You know, the other day when you left," Adrienne calls out to me after the visitor goes, "your mother was wide awake. W-i-d-e awake."

"Really?"

"As soon as you left, her eyes were wide open."

"I'll have to speak to her about that."

"How often do you come in?"

"A couple of times a week. She's almost always asleep."

"But she knows you're here," she says warmly.

"Maybe. Sometimes I think she does; other times, I'm not so sure."

"Well," she says, "you know what they say about mothers and their children. There's an invisible bond between them. She's aware of your presence. She knows you're here."

I nod and change the subject.

"Your job must be quite difficult," I say.

"How do you mean 'difficult'?"

"Dealing with people like Mrs. Henry and my mother. They're not all that talkative or active."

"I don't know if it's difficult," she replies, a bit unsure of herself. "I don't know if *difficult* is the right word. I love my job. I guess it is difficult to watch them suffering, but I love taking care of the elderly. I didn't always like it, sitting here like this, sometimes not doing much for hours. But over the years, I've come to like what I do and learn from it. You have to have patience. Some people might not realize it, but it's tiring, you know—tiring. You get stronger as time goes on. And I feel good about taking care of someone, giving them something they need, even if it's just a little quality of life. I feel good about that. It's tiring, though, sitting here watching someone sleep."

Suddenly, there's a loud noise just outside the door, a growl trying to form itself into words. Someone is having a tantrum.

"You must see a lot of people dying."

"A lot," she says with an ironic grin. "I've been chatting to people about ordinary things for twenty minutes, and then with the snap of a finger, they're gone. Just like that. One minute they're here, and the next they ain't. But you know, this job makes you appreciate life more. When you see people who used to be like you and me shouting their heads off or peeing into the radiator, it makes you realize you have to make the best of it while you can. Who knows what's going to happen?"

A doctor suddenly appears. He makes his way toward me because I have asked to see him. He is wearing a short-sleeved white shirt and dark blue pants, and he is shorter than I. His hair is black, and he wears glasses; his skin is pale, and his flesh is as soft as a woman's. After greeting me, he stands with his hands clasped over his crotch and a peace-be-with-you smile on his lips. He looks like a father-confessor. His name is Goodman.

"The nurse said you wanted to ask me some questions."

"Well, I just wanted to meet you and hear from you about my mother's condition."

"Your mother's function, as you already know, is very low. There's not much change in her condition from day to day. She's weak and on a feeder. So sometimes the feed regurgitates back up into the esophagus and gets into the airways. This causes some congestion in the lungs. Sometimes pneumonia. Not uncommon in cases like this. So we give her medication when that happens. Right now, she's on two drugs. One anti-seizure medication to prevent the recurrence of the stroke she had. Since she's had Alzheimer's, this is only to be expected. She's also on an antibiotic for her bedsores."

The white-haired Victor, with white woolen socks pulled up over his pajama bottoms, playfully toddles into the room, his footwear flopping like a seal's flippers. He takes hold of the trolley at the foot of my mother's bed as if he is going to give a lecture with my mother as his audience.

"Hi, Victor," Dr. Goodman says with a smile. "How are you today?"

"Not bad," Victor replies. "Are you okay?"

"I'm fine."

Nodding with satisfaction, Victor gives up his podium and leaves.

"Are there any particular questions you want to ask me or any comments you want me to pass on to the nurses?" the doctor asks.

"Not really," I reply. "I'm just concerned that when I come in here, she's so inactive—as if she's in a coma. She sleeps all the time and seems to be in pain. I'm just concerned about unnecessarily perpetuating that.

I've talked to her previous doctors about the prospect of intervention if anything should happen."

"There are four coded levels of intervention," he says authoritatively. "Red, yellow, blue, and green. Red is minimal intervention. If the patient catches pneumonia, for instance, we make her as comfortable as we can—put her on oxygen and keep her warm. But we give no antibiotics and engage in no invasive procedures. We do nothing else at this level. Yellow is moderate intervention, where we do all that we do at the red level but, in addition, assist her with drugs and antibiotics that are called for and tolerable in her situation. That's it, however. We make no effort to transfer her anywhere else for further treatment. I believe your mother is yellow."

"Yes, she is."

"If you feel comfortable with that, fine. If not and you want to change it to red, that's fine too. You can think about it. And if you want at any time to make that change, just inform us."

The doctor pays a visit to Mrs. Henry, who has been startled awake by the noise. My mother's Kangaroo beeper has gone off, and just beyond the door, the growler is having a barking match with someone equally inarticulate.

"Howat!"

"Ohen!"

"Howat!"

"Ohen!"

Dr. Goodman examines Mrs. Henry, urges her to rest, and tells her he'll be back later to make sure everything's all right. Meanwhile, Victor, the dotty nomad, is back—this time, mischievously lying down on Mrs. Garceau's empty bed. Within seconds, he's back up and off to someone else's room.

"I'm longing for home," Mrs. Henry says to Adrienne.

"You're longing for home? Home sweet home."

My mother's tongue hangs down over her bottom teeth. Her lips are twisted as if someone has just punched her in the mouth. Suddenly, she winces in pain several times in a row. I think about the levels of intervention: red, yellow, blue, green.

The man in the wheelchair worms his way past the door. Without using his hands on the control wheels or even making serious use of his legs, he propels himself by the power of his feet alone. His whole being is focused on this isolated movement, his entire energy concentrated on crawling a few inches at a time. His face is grave.

I kiss my mother's forehead and leave.

14

The Shield

I've been back to see my old stomping grounds in Newarthill a couple of times, to see the "glen" we played in, the filthy "burn" across which we built dams to swim in, the dead stumps that once were grand old oak trees—Big Annie and Queen Mary—the farmers' fields stretching out beyond this, and the graveyard near Holytown, where my friends and I would scamper around like a pack of wild dogs, hiding behind gravestones to frighten each other. In those days, it was all great fun, whereas now it seemed hopelessly small scale, drab, and nondescript. Nevertheless, for the Glascoe kids, it was an exhilarating release from the multitude of tensions at home.

Inside that home was something else. Whether it was from ordinary forgetfulness or the force of trauma, I had lost track of the many events Robert now talked about, even though they occurred during my childhood in the early 1950s. What he was going to tell me now would not only bring to light some of the mysteries of my parents' love life that I had no more than a dreamy recollection of, but also unexpectedly help me to make some sense of my own later romantic relationships, though this would be some time in coming.

"It was such an irony," Robert said, "that Dad's half brother, Johnny, admired him so much both before and long after these sad and peculiar times."

"What do you mean?" I asked my brother.

"Well, all I know is that something happened between Dad and

Johnny's wife, Molly. I was reeling from all the home stuff by now, and I really tried to tune it all out. So I'm short on details about this affair."

Suddenly, once again, a light went on in my head. An image from the distant past glowed brightly in my mind. My mother and I were standing at the bus stop on a lovely, sunny day, waiting for the Motherwell bus. When it came by, we didn't get on. "That's yer dad sittin' up there," she said, pointing to the upper deck of the bus. Sure enough, it was him. "He's been wi' that bitch Molly again!" She spat the words out. I was a boy seven or eight years old, and I had no idea what that meant. We had visited Uncle Johnny and Molly not long before this. I couldn't understand my mother's anger then, but now it became clear as day. Before I could fully register the significance of this, however, my brother was moving on to something else. He had reserved a group of stories like this one, it seems, until perhaps he thought I was ready to bear them.

"The most devastating event in my teenage life happened one afternoon as I was sitting in the kitchen, polishing my shoes. There was a knock at the front door. Mom, who was in the living room, reading a magazine, got up to answer. I just kept polishing my shoes, but I could see the woman through the window between the kitchen and the living room. I didn't think anything of this at first; it wasn't uncommon for Mom's neighbors and friends to drop in for a chat. But gradually, I realized that this mystery woman was talking about something serious. So I listened more carefully and heard a stunner: 'You and him—' the woman said without finishing her sentence. 'I know all about it. What right did you have? He's my husband. And you're a married woman, for pity's sake!' Mom had had it off with this woman's husband in a corridor, of all places, in the club!

"She denied the whole thing. I recall her saying—remember how with strangers she would put on good English?—'Nothing of the kind ever happened. I'm not that sort of woman.' Eventually, this woman left in tears. Mom said nothing to me, even though she must have realized I heard it all. She just slipped into her coat and disappeared out the door. I have no idea where you were. I don't know if you were exposed to that."

"No, I don't remember anything about it, but there were other things I'm beginning to recall that seem to fit the same pattern. Like the night I was wakened up sometime after midnight when an inexplicable commotion suddenly erupted among the houseful of guests who were at our place for a party. They were people from the club, and Molly's sister was there, but who else, I don't know. I just remember some vague, angry accusations and fighting words that frightened me and got my blood up. As people were spilling out the front door, I leaned out the window and shouted, 'Get out, and don't come back!'"

"You were very young then," my brother said, "so I can understand what you must have been going through. Did you know what happened?"

"I must have heard something disturbing if I yelled out the window, but I've blocked it out."

"Some guy in the group banged Mom in the bedroom cupboard!"

"Yeah," I said, "now that you say it, I seem to remember hearing talk of something like that."

The master bedroom, if it could be called that, had a large walk-in closet. It was used mostly for storing clothes, and a dresser was planted in front of it, blocking off the doors. It was easy to slide the dresser over, as I often did when Mom was mad at me. It was the closest thing to a secret compartment where I could easily hide or where even two adults could, I suppose, in drunken desperation, carry on—standing up, that is.

"There were other creepy incidents," Robert said. "I had already gone through some massive grief about Mom's loss of image when I walked in on her making out with another stranger. I think you were even in the bedroom, maybe asleep but there just the same. This happened more than once. I don't know if it was the same man each time, but eventually, it didn't matter to me. I developed a shield by that point and didn't care what was going on. I just ignored it because I'd seen it all before. I had become inured to the antics because they had become so normal. That shield was my protection," he said resolutely. After a pause, he picked up the thread. "Then there was the lodger."

"Yes, I have a vivid recollection of him," I said.

"He came from England, although how he ended up at our place, I'll never know. I mean, here we were, a family of two adults and two growing children living in a two-bedroom house, taking in a lodger!"

"Where did he sleep?"

"There was a sofa bed in the living room."

"What did we do for privacy?" I asked.

"There was none. I was flabbergasted at having to share our house with a total stranger. It was queer. It became even more so one time when I walked into the living room and he was standing uncomfortably beside Mom, who was sitting in the easy chair. Her hair was messed up, and the guy had lipstick all over his face. I could handle this by now, however, because it wasn't the first time. I had my shield. I didn't care. I never said that, but I thought it: *You can't hurt me now.* Then an incident happened late one night at our bedroom door, when you and I were lying in bed."

"Oh, yes," I said. It was coming back. "I remember that."

"You probably remember more than me. It never touched me. I think I'd dealt with losing my faith in both our parents by this point. I must have been fourteen or fifteen, and you—"

"Five or six."

"I stood there watching the whole thing. There was no emotional impact. But for you, that was a trauma. You must have been shattered. I remember you starting to cry."

"I was sitting up in the bed. I can still see you in your pyjamas with your hands behind your back, standing against the wall beside the bed. Dad was leaning in the doorway, gesturing in his vaguely threatening way while he spoke. Mom was in the unlit hallway behind him, and the lodger stood to her side, almost out of sight. 'Yer mither's leavin' us.' Dad was angry. 'She's goin' tae Londin wi' this guy here.' Mom, from the back, said, 'Robert, you bring Andy to Granny's tomorrow, okay?' Then they all disappeared, and you slipped back into bed. I remember you saying to me, 'What are you blubbering about?' Then I heard the door opening and Dad crying out Mom's name: 'Maggie, Maggie!'"

"I don't remember any of that. What happened next?"

"I don't know. I couldn't hear anything else after that. But we did go to Glasgow the next day."

"We did? I have no recollection."

"Oh, yes, I have photographic recall of Gran and me standing on the platform of Glasgow Central train station. We were watching Mom and the lodger kissing and hugging, he leaning out the train window, she reaching up from the platform. I even remember Gran saying, 'Oh, another wee kiss,' as she turned to take a peek at them. She was amazing with stuff like this. She seemed to be able to keep her head and carry on without recriminations for anyone. Clearly, by this time, she knew that Mom was not going, whereas I was still in the dark. My guess is that it was Gran who stopped it all and reminded Mom of her kids. I can't for the life of me recall my emotions, but I think I must have been relieved when the train began to leave and Mom was still standing there on the platform in her hat and coat, waving good-bye to her lover."

Robert was right—this incident had had a terrifying and long-lasting effect on me. Even when I spoke to him now, though, I still did not realize just how profound it was. The fallout would only be felt some years after this conversation—a good fifty-five years after the event, when I was to discover in a crisis with my wife, Adèle, that departures were traumatizing for me.

"When I look back on this stuff now," he said, "I wonder—what the hell were they thinking?"

Whatever trials and tribulations my brother and I had as children at the hands of our parents, I never felt I had the right to hold a grudge against or indulge in resentment toward either of them. My suffering simply did not seem to measure up to the trauma my father experienced during the war and not even to the miseries my mother endured. I knew full well that so much of the trouble between my parents, and between them and us, was a function of their bitter experiences. My mother once told me, "Your dad was a changed man after the war. He wasnae the man I married."

"Do you remember any of Dad's war stories?" I asked Robert, hoping for some insight.

"He never told them to me. But if you were in the right company, he would give an account in a kind of understated way. He talked about how in the thick of the Burmese jungle, the first strike of the match when lighting a cigarette was critical. He'd seen men killed for not realizing this—picked off by sharpshooting Japanese snipers. One story he told was about the time he and his mates were involved in a scramble after coming into contact with a Japanese squad. They dug themselves into position and started shooting. The Japanese launched a running attack; among the chargers was an unusually huge soldier. The British troops, including Dad, pummelled him with bullets, but he just kept coming. They were all shit scared. He was a giant among dwarfs, it seemed, and he appeared indestructible. They all heaved a huge sigh of relief when he finally keeled over just a few yards from their line of defence. Dad wrote about all this stuff in a notebook."

"I recall hearing about that notebook, but apparently one of his old army buddies got hold of it. I've never seen it."

"There's one other war-related event I want to tell you about before I forget. This happened not all that long ago. Dad was uncharacteristically talkative without being under the influence, so I was especially interested in what he was going to say. He told me that not long after he joined the forces, he and a friend were going through training, when the Chindit thing came along. He then said, 'We volunteered right away.' I remember thinking to myself, *Here I am, fifty-two years old, and I'm hurting like a child again at the hands of my father.* This man had a wife and kid! I cannot understand that."

Robert was clearly wounded even now. He was on the verge of slipping into a rage. I had not seen him like this often. Although he was in pain, he was beginning to piss me off.

"He had been called up, right?" I said. "Just to clarify."

"Yes," he answered a little impatiently. "But he *volunteered*," he went on, "to go off like that on a crazy suicide mission to Burma. It was outlandish! You would think that as a young man with a family, he would want to avoid being sent off like that, to not leave us. I was amazed at my reaction. I never knew that until he told me the story forty years after it happened. I don't even know if Mom knew. How could he do that? If you were in a parallel situation, how could you explain such a choice to Adèle and Ana?"

The force of his question came down on me like a hammer—not because it was appropriate, but just the opposite. I tried to keep my emotions in check because I was trying to listen to his voice. But it was almost inconceivable to me that he was oblivious to the circumstances of war in general, let alone this war in particular. Did he imagine that

Dad, who, as a former soldier who hated the life of the miner, was under no pressure to join the forces in the middle of the biggest and most destructive war in European history? Did he imagine that since this war was a world war—in fact, one being fought on multiple fronts—the old man would *not* be going off *somewhere* on *some* suicide mission to the Atlantic battleground or the Pacific? Did this nearly sixty-year-old, well-educated, grown-up son of Bob Glascoe not understand that as a mere pawn in the theatre of such a war, the old man had more or less *no choice* but to go and little or no choice on *where* to go? Maybe I was wrong about all this, but my brother had not even contemplated the possibility of such questions.

It seemed to me that our dad, and other jungle-seasoned men who had already fought in the Far East, were probably *sequestered* for a special duty in World War Two that required their specialized experience. They were more than likely all hand picked because of the particularity of their experience—in Dad's case, the experience he'd had in India with the Black Watch—to be transported off to Burma, where they were urgently needed. None of them were informed ahead of time about the nature of the battles they were "volunteering" to undertake. Their lives and the lives of their families were at the behest of the war makers and the generals in command.

"I couldn't explain or even make that kind of choice in the first place," I said in answer to his misplaced question, "but I'm not him, and I'm not likely to be in anything like the situation he was in. He was living in a very different time, in a wholly different situation."

I tried, in a rather bumbling way, to clarify what I was driving at, but I was so furious and so concerned about containing this fury that I didn't do a good job of changing his mind. I wanted to listen to Robert's story without prejudice, but I was struggling with what I saw as his own self-absorption and his indifference to his father's suffering.

"I'm not interested in rationalizing it," he retorted.

I was trying to control myself, and he was rubbing salt in the wound. Rationalizing! So that was how he saw my efforts to elicit from him a modicum of compassion and a smidgeon of sensitivity to and understanding of the plight of the old man. This little brother was hardly the one to enlighten him on that score. His own deep pain from childhood was still too much in evidence.

"He really hurt me," Robert continued. "He couldn't have hurt me more, I thought, and yet here he was doing it again—in my mature manhood, for God's sake, at such a late point in my life!"

My brother wasn't speaking as a mature man but as a wounded little boy, the one who had put up a shield to protect himself, to shut himself off all these years, and who now was still reacting to the perceived slight of long ago. It was time to get his own back, to unleash the fire of long-pent-up white-hot resentment and burn his parents to death.

He might have read something of my mood in my expression, because he suddenly changed his physical position to ease his discomfort and adopted a different tack, perhaps to allay his conscience.

"A lot of good things happened along the way. Once or twice, we went on a day trip to the seashore. Do you remember the holiday in Rothesay?"

I did remember Rothesay. Who could forget? Only the Scotch would consider Rothesay a holiday resort. It was, in those days, a dreary little place on the west coast of Scotland, with a continuously cold and damp climate. There was a sand beach but almost no sun, and if you dared to take a dip in the ocean, you would have to be treated for hypothermia afterward. I still have a photo of my brother on a beach of wet sand under a dark, cloudy sky, standing against the sea wall in his short trousers and "fair isle" sleeveless woolen jumper, looking for all the world as if he would rather be anywhere else. So I was surprised to learn that there had been something good about Rothesay. Although, again, Robert's idea of good was a curious mixture of everything but.

"For the old man to go on a trip like this was unheard of, although I don't remember doing anything with him—or with Mom, for that matter. I remember going to a film by myself—*Death of a Salesman*—which I hated."

Again, I had to bite my tongue. Talk about living on different planets—here was the aeronautics engineer turned literary critic now trashing one of the classics of twentieth-century drama and one of my favourite plays! I could easily have defended it against his lame criticisms, but I reminded myself once more that this was Robert's story. So I

119

pondered in silence the irony that the play is largely a father-and-son tragedy and, even more so, the irony of Robert's memory of it in one of his "good" childhood stories!

The only worthy thing this film gave him was a cigarette he found on the way out of the theatre: "I had just started smoking. In those days, it was a bit subversive. Mom and Dad didn't know. But you knew."

"Because I was there," I said. "I can still see the two of us on that dull, wet, rainy day, shivering in the close of the apartment house we were boarding in—you lighting up, me watching you with envy. You said, 'Don't you tell Ma.' The first thing I did when I went back to the rooms was to tell: 'Ma, Robert's smokin' in the close!' I'll never forget the look on her face. 'Oh, is he now? I'll have tae have a wurd wi'im when he comes in.' But she could barely conceal her amusement at your mischief and my childish giving away of your secret."

Robert did talk about some of the other good things in his childhood. Mostly these things involved going to soccer games with his uncles, staying with Gran, and getting up to mischief with friends in the glen. All of this was a perfunctory effort to balance the picture of his unbroken childhood misery, the responsibility for which he laid squarely at the feet of our parents.

The absence of Auld Angus, my grandfather McGregor, in this picture was so gaping a hole that I had to ask Robert to tell me about him. I had heard some stories about him from my mother and suspected he was responsible for something quite sinister. Exactly what, I wasn't sure.

"What do you know about the split in the family?" I asked.

Robert knitted his brow, perplexed. "I don't know of any split." His remembrance of his earliest experiences was remarkable. His forgetfulness of some things I knew all too well was clearly a defense mechanism. The shield he had created as a child still protected him.

"It was right there when I was a boy, from the earliest times," I said. "There was a big game going on, one I more or less had to play a part in. The game was favorites. Granpa favored Uncle Don and his wife, Amy, and their kids; Granny favored Mom, Dad, you, and me. I grew up with that reality. I always put it down to the antipathy between Mom and her dad."

"I don't remember anything about Granpa other than his attempt to be a nice old gentleman to a little boy like me—his first and, for a long time, only grandkid."

It was during moments like these that Robert's attitude simply floored me. Our experiences of our grandfather could not have been more opposed. Even worse, he blithely carried on talking as if my questions and suggestions were so far out that they hardly warranted serious discussion, as if they were merely the wayward musings of a still-so-little brother. But here I was, blaming him again for his reactions as a child. I had to remind myself for the umpteenth time that he was just recounting his childhood experience at face value. I bit my tongue once again.

"I certainly don't remember Mom having any problem with Granpa," he said. "My impression is that she loved her father. So whatever happened between them, if anything did, must have happened later."

He spoke with such assurance that I wanted to launch into an argument to convince him otherwise, until it occurred to me—again—that this was the child speaking in the voice of the man. I let his story tumble out. But I couldn't stop myself from feeling that what followed were all euphemisms that just rolled off his tongue.

"I know that Auld Angus and his son, our uncle Don, had a symbiotic kind of relationship," he said. "Granpa liked a drink, and he was aggressive—a bad combination, to be sure. To be honest with you, if you consider his background ... Well, you know what Glasgow was like. You look at anyone the wrong way and you're a dead man. He'd learned how to handle himself. He got into fights at the pub, and it was Uncle Don's job to go and fish him out."

For some reason, my brother was showing incredibly uncharacteristic understanding here—understanding of one who deserved it less than the others whom he was *dis*inclined to show it toward.

"I only remember good times with Granpa McGregor. He and Uncle Don took me on a trip one time in Don's old 1940s Morris. We travelled to Dumfries."

I remembered this trip too, but it only reinforced the fact of the split—rather than the opposite, as Robert was suggesting. Uncle Don, Auld Angus, and Don's son drove up to our door in Newarthill to pick

Robert up. I told my mother I wanted to go along. Don was firm in his refusal: "There's nae room!" He was right—there were five seats in the car, including the driver's, and that was that. I ran to the bathroom to bawl my eyes out, but I could hear my mother trying to persuade Don to take me. He eventually agreed. But neither he nor Grandfather wanted me along, and they made no bones about showing it. I had to sit on Robert's knee throughout the entire trip.

We drove along the narrow roads that rolled up and down the heather-covered Dumfrieshire hills. This was the first time I had seen that part of Scotland, and there was something of Laurel and Hardy about the journey that made it memorable in an odd kind of way.

"Once, when the car stalled going up a hill—" my brother said, snorting with laughter.

"We all got out to push it up!" I said, finishing his sentence.

We laughed heartily at the remembered image. The object of the trip seemed to be to end up in Sanquar, the birthplace of Auld Angus. I don't have much recollection of anything else except the landscape and the feeling of being an outsider on the trip.

"We went into a place with a fireplace and a bar," Robert said. "Six or seven locals were happy to see us. This was a place where you met your friends, and if strangers came in, all the better. We played dominoes with them, Granpa had his pint, and you had one of those horrible Scotch soft drinks, Tizer or Irn Bru! I'd never really been much in pubs, and I never liked them. Glasgow pubs were out of the question. But this one was different."

So there had indeed been some good times in Robert's early growing up in Scotland. I asked the inevitable question: "What made you leave for Canada?"

"Do you remember the day I left?"

Remember it? How could I forget? It had followed a going-away party at which, in those days, everyone was expected to sing. Robert fancied himself a kind of Sinatra and sang a pretty good rendition of "Love Is a Many-Splendored Thing." I can still recall the lyrics: "Love is nature's way of giving a reason to be living ..."

He couldn't have sent a more ironic message than this, although none of it came home to me as a nine-year-old boy. His leave taking was another traumatic moment in my young life. Not because I was close to Robert—I wasn't. Just as Dad was largely absent and silent in his life, Robert was largely absent and silent in mine, a fact he never acknowledged. The old man wasn't absent this time, though, but was right there on the dockside to see his older son off. Neither he nor Robert shed a single tear.

Mom was bawling her eyes out, and so was I—not so much for my brother perhaps, but more likely because it reminded me all too much of the earlier near breakup of the family. This time, it was actually happening. I stood there waving a brightly colored handkerchief Robert had given me for my birthday. I could see him and his friend leaning over the stern of the ship. I waved until I was no longer able to make them out.

"Mom asked me," my brother said, shaking his head, "'Was it something I did?' I had no intention of hurting her at this late stage of the proceedings. So I said no. I couldn't honestly say yes anyway, because at that age, I would have left for other reasons. I was up for military service, and although I had some interest in joining the RAF, I wasn't about to allow myself to be drafted into the army. I had designs on Canada anyway. Betty was already living there, and she'd encouraged me on her last visit. In fact, by the time I was fifteen, I made up my mind that I was going the year I turned eighteen."

"You leaned over and whispered to me," I reminded him, "'Look after Mum for me, will you?'"

"Did I?"

His request then had completely bewildered me. I didn't know how I was to look after her or why, although I had the vague sense that she needed protection from my father. I didn't say this to my brother now, though. He was beginning to get restless again.

Even at the best of times, Robert was always uncomfortable. He needed to take regular breaks from sitting, and during these breaks, he would frequently eat a bowl of blueberries. It was one of the few alternative therapies he seemed to be convinced of. He had heard that blueberries were a good antioxidant, so he was eating them by the bushel. I was horrified at this because I suspected that this painful condition was the result of some factor in his environment that he was unaware of, and he was gobbling non-organic blueberries, which were among the most pesticide-infested of all fruits! I told him all this, but on this score, I would always be the baby brother babbling about nothing of any consequence. Our conversations around this were brief and tense. I needed the walks on the beach as much as he did.

Although I didn't know it when we returned from one of our walks on the beach, Robert's story was drawing to a premature close. The reasons for this were predictable and would soon become clear. When we sat down on the balcony of his apartment again, he picked up where he'd left off with the saga of our father.

"After they came to Canada," he said of Maggie and Bob, "there was some opening up. The old man seemed to become an odd kind of dad."

"How do you mean?"

"One incident brought this home to me. One morning, not long after Elaine and I moved into the Clarkson house, I had just gotten out of bed around eight o'clock. I was stretching and looked out the front window. There was the old man, walking up the driveway. It was unnerving. He figured he could come over anytime. But I didn't want to stop that. I thought, *Maybe I'm gonna have a dad after all.* But while you used to be able to drop in on neighbors anytime in Scotland, you just didn't do that here. If he ever wanted to see Alex Baines, who lived just across the street in Newarthill, he just went. He didn't send me to see if Alex was there. And if Alex wasn't up, he'd get him up. Now he was doing the same thing here. I had the distinct feeling that if I hadn't opened the door, he would just have walked in. I don't know if you were aware that he was doing it."

"Did he do it more than once?"

"Oh yeah. Yes! He would suddenly appear unannounced and would have walked right in the door if we hadn't started locking the door."

"This must have been on weekends," I said.

"Mostly, but he came anytime there were holidays as well."

"You know that Mom worked on weekends?" I said by way of explanation.

"Yeah, I guess he just wanted to hang out. But it just wasn't practical or quite the right thing to do with a young couple. I think I succeeded in getting that across to him. I wanted him to call before he came, to find out what we were doing."

"Maybe it was his crude attempt," I said in an effort to fill in the picture for a brother who should have known better, "to plug up the hole in his family life after all these years. Maybe it was the act of a desperate man who lacked the social graces to carry it out in a more appropriate way. You may be interested to know that he and Mom, a bit later, did the same thing with Maria and me when we were going to university in Guelph. They would land at our place every single weekend without thinking about anything else we might want to do. I didn't want to tell them not to do this, because I knew that having made the move to Canada—a move they were unprepared for and unequipped for so late in their lives—they were now without any friends at all. They had become alienated from you and Elaine. Their out-of-sync work weeks, with him on perpetual night shift in that miserable packing job and her working days and weekends, meant they barely even had each other for company. They were lonely and miserable."

Robert hadn't seen any of this, nor was he interested now. He'd had too many of his own worries to worry about theirs.

"Well, I guess that's all I have to tell you. You know the rest anyway."

His life story ended, it seemed, when he was eighteen, give or take a few years. My frustration with his obduracy made me probe into it more and ask the question Robert had all along intended to avoid.

"There's one more thing that I wanted to ask you about. This is the most obvious thing and, at the same time, the most sensitive—you haven't mentioned it at all."

My brother got up from his seat, presumably to ease his persistent discomfort.

"Mom's relationship," I continued, "with Elaine."

He walked over to the counter between the kitchen and the living room. He stood there for a few moments with his back to me, leaning on the counter, shifting his weight from one side to the other to relieve his discomfort.

"If you don't want to talk about it, don't," I added, "but the relationship had such an influence on all of our lives, really. It seemed to be doomed from the beginning. It doesn't loom large in my life now, because it was all so long ago, but it did at one time. And I would like to understand what Mom's role in all that was."

I walked over beside him. His face was flushed, and his eyes were on fire. The touchy subject had been touched, and it was red hot.

"I wasn't about to break up my family," he said with barely subdued fury.

The irony of this oblique answer to my question did not occur to him. Who was the "family" he was referring to? Our family—his and mine with Bob and Maggie—or his family—he and Elaine and young Bobbie?

"Don't worry to say anything then," I said to calm him down.

But he went on anyway to understate the case so dramatically that it amounted to a serious distortion of that history.

"All I wanna say about it is that it was a very difficult time for me, and yes, it was a bit disappointing. For a long time, I never understood it myself, but I was determined that it wasn't going to keep Mom and Dad from my family—or at least from my children. Eventually, things came around, and it turned into a non-issue."

I could hardly believe my ears. The shield of bygone days was still at work. There never was a time that the animosity between my mother and Elaine was a non-issue.

"Elaine explained it to me years later. You have to understand that she was very young, twenty-three or something, and she looked up to Mom. So when she had the baby, Bobbie, she was devastated by Mom's behavior. She had a painful birth. The doctors did X-rays and discovered that Bobbie was on his side and wouldn't come out. Elaine had to endure a caesarean. She was in the hospital days before the birth and didn't come home for several days. She expected and didn't get a mother figure to help her then. She thought she had built up a relationship with Mom and Dad—but they never once went into the hospital to hold her hand, to see her, or even just to offer sympathy. They didn't ask after her health or what the baby weighed.

"Elaine had nobody on her side when it really mattered. When I thought about this years later, I figured Dad was less to blame than Mom, because he probably felt it was not a man's call to make. It was just so like Mom not to be there when it counted. I know they were stressed out by the situation with you and Maria, but even that doesn't justify their obvious lack of concern."

The "situation" Robert was referring to was my bungled marriage with Maria, the deeply embarrassing situation of two shy teenagers being forced to endure a wedding ceremony so ludicrous it could only have been engineered by desperate or loopy parents. What made matters even more pathetic for Robert—or, more precisely, for Elaine, herself giving birth at the same time—was that our child was born one day before theirs.

Either Robert had convinced himself over the years since that his abridged story was true, or he was being disingenuous. The trouble between my mother and Elaine started long before the birth of our children, and it burgeoned into a bitter conflict, which eventually included me. Elaine was driven to distraction by her insecurity about my brother's affections being redirected away from her to other members of his family and old friends. One by one, they were all sent packing. She had told my first girlfriend a cock-and-bull story about me throwing back in her face a dinner she had lovingly made for me. That relationship, not surprisingly, never got off the ground.

She tried the same thing a year or two later with Maria, whom she met one day in a shopping mall. Had Robert forgotten that I actually made a special trip to Clarkson one day to confront him about this? Perhaps it was a case of the forgetfulness that was a kind of blanking of the slate, the necessary condition of all future actions. Whatever it was with my brother's memory, we just stopped talking—then and now.

That story and the present one were over. Our conversation was ended. It was time for another walk, nothing more than chitchat. We drove back to Houston the next day, and I saw Robert only rarely after that.

The distance between us wasn't just geographical.

15
Slow-Motion Horror Film

"Hello? Eleanor from 8 West speaking," says the voice on the other end of the phone.

"Yes?" I answer apprehensively, as I always do when I receive these late-night telephone calls from Riverdale.

"The doctor thought that your mother's breathing was labored. So she's now on antibiotics. The pneumonia has set in again."

"Is she on oxygen?"

"Yes. And she's stable at the moment."

"Okay. I'll be in tomorrow morning."

"Yes, I think that would be best."

It's more painful than usual to see her when I get there. She's wearing a clear plastic mask hooked up to an oxygen tank. It covers her nose and mouth. She's taking quick, short breaths. Her chest is heaving with the effort. Her hands are blue, and her arms are cold and damp with sweat.

I admire her but am filled with sadness. How can I think of taking her off the antibiotics? At least they give her a fighting chance.

Thirty seconds later, I'm lamenting the decision to put her on the medication. My benign Zen monk and the ferocious madman are itching to get into this conversation, but I'm determined to keep them out.

How many more times can she sustain this? How often should I help her to endure this agonizing struggle?

This is the fourth time in the last eighteen months she's been hit with pneumonia. The fourth time she's been given oxygen. The fourth time she's been pumped up with antibiotics. And for what? She's struggling with every ounce of energy just to breathe, struggling for each breath so that she can take the next one. That's it.

"Hi," Connie says when I go into the nurse's office for a report. "Have a seat. I almost called you yesterday."

"I eventually received a call from Eleanor."

"Yes, I know, but I thought she was going to go."

Her grim expression abruptly changes to a grin when an orderly interrupts to drop off some coffee cups he had promised her.

"You're good at this," she chirps.

"Is that enough?"

"Yes, thanks," she says with a smile.

She turns her attention to me again with an appropriately changed look on her face. I can only admire how these nurses are like actors, masters of the diplomacy of expression. I suppose it comes from simultaneously accommodating the wild behaviors of demented patients and relentless queries of hyper-anxious families.

"She was so blue; I thought she was going to go. But she looks better now."

"She still looks a little blue to me."

"She was much worse this morning. Tammy was up to see her. You just missed her. She waited for a while, in fact, to see you."

"Tammy?"

"Yes, she's the new doctor on the floor. Dr. ... I'm not sure what her last name is. It's hard to pronounce. I just call her Tammy."

"I'd like to see her if she comes back."

"I can page her."

"No, it's fine. If I don't see her today, I'll be back in tomorrow."

A man sounds as if he's making a point of letting everyone know he's retching in the hallway, but he's just attempting to make words out of incoherent sounds. He does this repeatedly. When he's really excited, he sounds like a constipated grizzly trying to shit.

Back at my mother's bedside, I alternately marvel at and bewail how she has been so near the edge so many times yet pulled back before going over. What's holding her here is anyone's guess—perhaps that thread she

129

talked about many years ago. But you have to wonder what the appeal is in the life she's got left to live. Surely death is a better option than what she has now. Maybe. How am I to judge?

"Wake up, Marjorie," Adrienne calls out to Mrs. Henry. "Your lunch is here."

"Wake up, Marjorie," I say under my breath, "and then go back to sleep. Yes, Marjorie, this is quality of life."

I think about all the labor, energy, expertise, and emotion we focus on "assisting" the dying. It's not the fact that's troubling but the results—what we call "quality of life." I'm sick of the damn phrase. I'm sick of the reality in my mother's case.

I can't help thinking that I'm part of it, part of a collective exercise in prolonging the agony of the last moments of life. We reduce it to a set of movie frames to be considered one at a time, just to make sure everything that can be done is being done and that all due consideration has been given. We don't seem to have noticed that the slow-motion production is a horror film that no one wants to appear in—least of all, I cannot help but think, the person at the center of it.

The man of grunts and groans in the wheelchair is making his usual rounds from room to room. There's a faintly wry smile on his face as he tries to pull himself into my mother's room by the doorframe. An attendant, however, grabs him from behind. For the first time since I've made his acquaintance, he utters something coherent.

"What the fuck are you doing?"

"Come on, John," she says, gently but firmly prying his fingers loose.

"No, no, no!" he cries before he deteriorates into his customary incoherence.

"We have somewhere else to go," she insists.

Where do we go from here, John? I wonder. *Where do we go from here?*

The Zen monk has heard me, and so has the madman. This time, they barge in together. Looking for all the world like Abbot and Costello, they make a rare joint appearance.

"It's time," the madman growls.

"You have to let go, son, sometime," the monk chimes in with an air of overweening sympathy.

"You two agree on something?" I ask.

"She's already gone," the madman barks. "You're the one who's pumping oxygen through her lungs."

"You wonder why she's hanging on," the monk says softly, "but it's you who's hanging on to her."

"You're the one who's got her hooked up to all this machinery," the madman hisses. "Just the kind you've been swearing against for years. Isn't this an exercise in artificial life support? Aren't you the one who made the decision to prolong the struggle you lament about?"

"She wants to go," the monk whispers. "Look at her—look at the struggle she's enduring. It's not the desire to stay that's keeping her here but the fear of leaving. She wants to go. She's just afraid."

"You're mother's out of her mind, kid—pure and simple," the madman contests. "She hasn't a clue about what she's doing. She's brain dead—figuratively, if not literally. You should give her a little helping hand to go the whole way. That's all."

"Say your good-byes," the monk says, mouthing the words almost inaudibly as he evaporates out the window.

"Change the colour code from yellow to red," the madman rasps. "Pull the plug, buddy; it's over."

As the madman fades into oblivion once again, a workman's drill erupts down the hall. The lady with the chainsaw voice responds in kind. I have to leave before I go nuts.

"So you're off?" Adrienne asks.

"I'll be back tomorrow."

"She has no other family?"

"I'm the only regular visitor."

"Don't they live here?"

"One does; the others don't."

"She knows you're here."

"I wonder."

"There's nine of us in our family," Adrienne tells me. "My mom used to say, 'I love all nine, but if one shows up, that's enough.' You're doing the best you can. That's enough for her. And that's what counts up above."

It's a kind thought, meant to comfort. But the Zen monk in me

131

squirms at the useless theology, and the madman cackles like the crazy woman in Jane Eyre's attic.

"Thanks, Adrienne. I'll see you tomorrow."

16
Spinning

There was something serendipitous about my cousin Eileen's invitation to attend her wedding in Saskatchewan in the summer of 1997. I had been hankering to go to Saskatchewan anyway to see her mom, Aunt Betty, and to talk to her about my mother and our family. I had known Eileen from her first visit to Scotland in the 1960s and had seen her occasionally since. She had come to visit me in Vancouver following the breakup of her first marriage to a computer analyst. Eileen was now marrying a farmer, and I thought he might prove a better match for her. Even though she was a university graduate and a social worker, she came from a farm herself, and the land was still in her bones.

Her mother was my mother's younger sister by two years. She had been a war bride. Having met and married a Canadian RAF pilot, Bill Robinson, she left for Canada in 1946. The shift from Glasgow to the small prairie town of Stoughton must have been a radical change for her. Robinson worked on the O'brien farm, one of the largest in the area, sprawling over many square miles. Though Betty gave birth to a son in the first year, the marriage didn't last. She was an attractive almost-blonde woman with a cheerful demeanor. Tough and wiry, she was nobody's fool and had a spine of steel. A profoundly honest woman with a sharp wit and strong sense of decency, Betty carried a lot of weight in the community. She had been used to working hard in Glasgow and did what she had to do after her divorce, which was to take on odd jobs about town and on the surrounding farms to make a living for her and the new child.

Eventually, she remarried. The man was Pat O'brien, Robinson's former boss, who, along with his brother Gord, carried on a long family tradition of tending the same chunk of land for generations. Pat was a man of the soil and had a heart of gold. A gritty, decent, and witty man, he worked the land himself well into his eighties. With the O'briens, Betty had married into a tradition.

Adèle and I were going to be the odd couple out at the O'brien family wedding ceremony. We were, after all, urban types from the despised East and a racially mixed couple. We wondered how everyone was going to take this in the farming community of Edenwold, but we soon discovered we didn't have to worry about a thing. When we arrived late the night before the wedding, looking for Eileen's farm, we were met at what turned out to be the reception hall for the wedding ceremony by a woman who had been one of Eileen's rivals for the affections of her new husband-to-be and who, true to prairie form, was taking responsibility for organizing the ceremony! She was delighted to meet us. She insisted that we have a drink with her at the local watering shed, which was just that—a corrugated tin shed with a bar, a few fold-up tables, and one or two curious patrons. In a matter of minutes, we were clued in to the comings and goings of Eileen and her husband-to-be, Doug, not to mention everyone else in town.

Eventually, we reached the farm, having been carefully guided there by our new friends. Eileen was an intelligent splinter of a girl with a big heart. She had the virtue of always looking as if she were the same age, much younger than the thirty-something she was supposed to be. In fact, she still looked like the sixteen-year-old I had taken to an acid rock concert on one of her visits to Toronto, the same girl I had skied with a few years later on Whistler Mountain. I think she was happy some out-of-towners were coming, because her heart was still split between the farm and the city. She had gotten a taste of the latter in her university years and subsequent work in Regina. Her new partner was a strapping man about Eileen's age, someone I had met on a brief trip they made to

Toronto a few years before. He was not only open-minded enough to understand Eileen's tension but seemed to embrace it.

We thought we might be late for the ceremony because we had only the locals' informal directions to guide us, and those were not for the uninitiated. But nobody got lost in the prairies. From a distance, we could see the spire of the little Anglican church glistening in the sun. The church stood on the only mound resembling a hill in the expanse of flatness all around us. When we arrived, we were ushered into the cosy little church and were immediately surrounded by welcoming faces and polite nods. I thought about how presumptuous we had been, Adèle and I, worrying so much about ourselves being a spectacle, when the minister walked up to the altar—the first ordained woman I'd ever seen.

The bride and groom arrived and took their places, kneeling before the minister. Suddenly, the congregation all began to laugh, to the delight of the minister, although she had no idea what was going on. Bride and groom turned to see what the commotion was about. Someone had painted a few words on the soles of the groom's shoes: "Please save me." This unique ceremony was followed by a reception that I had to agree was a barrel of laughs—everybody here knew everything about everybody else and wasn't afraid to tell. This turned out to be the most entertaining wedding I'd ever been to.

In the evening, back at the farm, Betty and I sat down to talk. She had been a smoker all her life and was now suffering from serious emphysema. Well into her seventies, she was afflicted by a wet, chesty cough that sounded as if her lungs were altogether breaking up. It was clear that she did not have long to go. But you'd never guess from her spirit. She was cheerful and alert, easygoing and blunt, as I had always known her to be.

I had been fond of Betty since the first time I met her, between her marriages at Gran's place in Glasgow, on her first visit back to Scotland in the 1950s. Her son was about my age, and we played together in the old war shelters behind Gran's tenement flat. One day, a local girl invited all the kids to come into her house to watch television, which none of us had ever seen before. Everyone was invited but my cousin and me, because we were outsiders. When I went back inside and told Betty this, she leaped out of her seat, grabbed our hands, and led us upstairs to the girl's flat, the door of which was wide open because there were so many kids sitting on the floor, watching TV. Betty pulled us through the doorway and announced, "They're here to see the television too." No one said a word, and we sat there happily with everybody else.

"What do you want me to tell you?" Betty asked.

"Whatever you remember about your life with my mom. Whatever you would like to say."

She started off as if she were going to sum everything up in one or two sentences.

"Your granpa was pretty strict with us kids in the early days. Your mom had to fight to go to her first dance when she was sixteen. A couple of years later, I got to go without a fight. I missed my bus home. I didn't get to another dance after that for a long time. Your mom loved the dancin', but that's all she did for fun. She never had any interest in sports. Granpa had a motorcycle and sidecar, and when your dad started coming around, Granpa and him used to go off riding."

"Dad used to love telling the story of a trip they took to Dumfries," I said. "It was like something out of an old W. C. Fields film. They were ripping down one of those steep braes in the rolling, heather-covered hills, Dad on the cycle and Granpa—or Auld Angus, as Dad used to call him—in the sidecar, when the one separated from the other. Dad didn't notice till he got to the bottom of the hill that Granpa had sailed off into a grassy field. Luckily, nobody was hurt. They went off to the local pub for a pint and a laugh."

"Yeah, there were some good times," Betty said, taking this as a cue to tell me about another, perhaps to allay the effect of what was to come. "One night, Mom and Dad went to the pictures with my younger brother, your uncle Andrew. Your dad had an Alsatian dog, which was staying at Saracen Street while he was away at the war. It had seven pups. Mom and Dad said they'd take the key, but I insisted that they just leave it and bring me a bottle of Irn Bru when they came home. I was going to stay up and play with the pups by the fireside. I did for a while, and then I started to doze off. I just went to bed and fell sound asleep. The next thing I heard was the Irn Bru cap being opened by my ear. Mom,

Dad, Uncle Andrew, your mom, and seven-year-old Robert had all come home, but they were unable to unlock the door or rouse me. They had to call the local fire brigade to help them pick the lock and let them in! Boy, was your mom sore at me that night!"

Betty laughed herself into a fit of coughing.

"Your mom was hard to please. She never just fell in with somebody; she chose her friends carefully. Your mom met your dad when she was sixteen. They got married quickly, but it was never a happy marriage. They were always arguing. Whether your dad ever hit your mother, I don't think so. They were both really jealous. Your mom liked the dancin', and your dad didn't. This caused a lot of tension. During the war years, she went dancin' a lot. She didn't go to see men or anything, but she just loved the dancin'. There was nobody else but Bob for your mom."

Betty began cautiously, perhaps because she wasn't sure how I was going to take it. Gradually, though, she relaxed and became more candid.

"When your dad went to the war, they wrote back and forth. They even argued in their letters. He would write something about her running around, and she would get mad."

"The whole family lived in the Saracen Street flat," I said. "How was that?"

"We all lived there, even Amy after she got married to your uncle Don. Amy and your mom never got along. Robert was a nice, quiet child. He was like me, wanted to stay out of the way of all the fightin'."

Amy was coming to the house as Don's girlfriend and ended up staying as his wife. I only knew her in later years as an unattractive dark-haired woman with a cruel streak and a perpetually vile expression. She was always attacking her kids.

"Tell me more about Mom and her fighting ways."

"Your mom was brilliant."

I was happy to know that at least one other person in the family besides myself felt this way. My mother, who'd had no formal education beyond high school, had frequently surprised me over the years with her unexpectedly incisive comments.

"She and Don were twins and went to school at the same time. Don was no dummy, but before you knew it, she had jumped two grades ahead of him. When she got to high school, she shone again. In them days, not just anybody could go to university. You had to be recommended by your school. And that was really somethin'. Your mom received that recommendation. This meant she had to go to Edinburgh, I think, for an exam. She and your granpa set out for the train. Well, they missed it. Granpa said, 'We'll take the bus.' But she refused. 'We'll wait for the next train,' she said. I don't know why she did such a thing. Anyway, she was late for the exam, and they wouldn't let her sit. But they scheduled another time for her to come back. Your mom wouldn't go back."

"Why not, for God's sake?"

"I don't know. She was just so strong-headed. She wouldn't compromise with anybody when she made up her mind about something."

Betty was on a roll now.

"Everything about your mom was absolutes. She was very possessive."

"About what?"

"Robert. Robert was hers, no one else's. Even though we all loved him and looked after him, she possessed him. And Granny. She possessed Granny. The two of them belonged to your mom."

"This must have been hard on you and the others at Saracen Street."

"No, it was fine with me. I just accepted things the way they were. But your mom never got along with Father. Don and I were more on his side than she was. With Mother, it didn't make a difference. Maggie was more possessive. Mom and Robert belonged to her; Dad, in her mind, belonged to us. This didn't really suit Robert, even as a little boy. In the early days of the war, when she would sometimes go off at weekends to the Cleland house because all her friends were there, Robert was always happy to go with her. But he was sure happy to get back to Gran's afterwards."

Betty told her story in a matter-of-fact way, without a hint of resentment or accusation in her voice. She was blunt about the things that didn't thrill her and gracious about what she loved and respected in her sister.

"Your mom was brilliant at everything she did. When eventually she got the job at Mains' and the weekends in Cleland more or less came to a halt during the war, she always did things properly and really well. She became head crane driver, which meant that she had all the bigger stuff."

"Lifting steel girders and moving other heavy metal equipment across the factory floor?"

"Yeah."

"So you saw Mom at work?"

"I worked there too for a few months. I'd been on a job for five years until the factory folded. Your mom told me, 'If you want a job, just go see Rankin.' So I went to see him. He asked me, 'Are you Betty Glascoe?' I said no. So he said, 'Well, we don't have any jobs.' Back at home, Maggie scolded me. 'You had an appointment with Rankin today, and you never went.' 'I did,' I said. 'He told me there were no jobs.' Talk about mistaken identity! I laughed when I realized his mistake."

"He got your name wrong, thinking that yours was the same as her married name."

"It was his fault as well as mine, but oh, your mom was really hot-headed about that."

My mother's pull was impressive. She once told me that none of the men ever dared insult her. I had thought that this was because she was tough, smart, and articulate; had a comeback for everybody; and could cuss and swear with the best of them. I think it was all of the above, but there was more. Betty shed new light on this old story.

"She had an affair with Rankin," she suddenly said, as if to explain all this. "But it was still your dad for her," she added quickly, just in case I was worried.

I wasn't. The veils had been lifted from my eyes. My mother, it seemed to me now, had been spinning in the same grooves all her life. I began to think of my own dalliances with other women outside my marriages. Was I just repeating her patterns? Had her past become my future? This question popped into my head many times on this journey, a journey into the past that wasn't really past at all but alive and well in the present.

"Those were the war years," I said, as if this were the answer to all such divergences from the norm.

"She brought him up to the house a few times. Gran wasn't too happy, but she just went along with anything your mom did. I don't know how it all ended up when your dad wrote that he was coming home."

"How did you get along with Mom?"

"I used to run away with her clothes. She had such pretty dresses. Maggie was good about that kind of stuff. We got along all right in those days, but we had different views on life. I accepted things as they were. She wanted to change them. I didn't dispute things. She'd argue with a fly! Don and I got along good."

"Why didn't she get along with her father?"

"Your granpa drank and ran around with other women. Your mom and Gran would talk about this but never let me in on it."

"You were the younger sister. Did you ever see any of this stuff?"

"Yeah, I saw a lot and overheard things. It started before we lived on Saracen Street. I was probably about ten, and we were still in Fife, where your mom and I were born. One day, somebody said we were going to the station to meet Dad's sister. So we all trotted down to greet the 'sister' coming off the late-afternoon train. She was about twenty-one. She'd had a baby with Granpa. And Granny accepted this. She was there with us. Don't ask me why. I don't know how long this woman stayed—"

"You mean she lived with you?"

"Oh yeah, she lived with us all right. She may even have slept in Granpa's bed. Granny just accepted it. I don't know how long she was there."

"So my mom would have been about twelve. How did she take all this?"

"Your granpa would come in drunk, and your mom would argue with him."

"Even then, at that early age."

"Yeah, she was strong-headed."

I never got the impression that Betty used this word in a positive sense. She was a deeply fair-minded person, but the phrase was a euphemism for a far-less-flattering description of a sister she both loved and disliked. I, however, was beginning to wonder if I was getting close to the heart of my mother's troubled life. At the age of twelve, she was already standing up for her mother and the whole family against her graceless and audaciously bawdy father.

"That's how she got into trouble with him."

"Was there any physical abuse on his part?"

"No. Granpa liked to drink, but like I said, I don't think he ever hit a woman in his life."

"You were a witness to more than one of Granpa's escapades?"

"Once when we were on Saracen Street—I was about eighteen years old—a telegram came for Gran. Granpa was working in England. He was on his way home from London after being away for months, and a lady friend was coming with him. 'A lady friend,' Gran said. 'Well now, who would that be?' Don shrugged his shoulders and volunteered to go to Glasgow Central to meet him. I went along with him. I can still see my dad, his lady friend behind him, stepping down from the train, a handsome man with thick dark hair, dressed in his pin-striped blue suit and tie, his black Manhattan fedora, and his black-and-white swing shoes polished to the hilt."

"Sounds like a working-class dandy," I said. "Now I know what all those London pay packets were spent on."

"He met this woman in London and invited her to Glasgow for a visit. I don't remember anything else being said. I have no idea now how long she stayed. I wondered what made my mother accept all this, but I could never say anything like that then. Didn't know any better. I never looked down on my father at the time."

Betty coughed as if she were going to expire and then suddenly stopped and carried on as if nothing were the matter.

"Then there was the Amy affair," she said cryptically.

Amy, Don's girlfriend, was, at that time, a slim, bony girl with dark hair and slender legs. At nineteen, she was already manipulative, bad tempered, and rough mannered. She had enough hold over Don, who was a year older, that she was able to inveigle her way into this more-than-permissive household to be treated more or less like one of the family.

"Amy and I were like this," Betty said, crossing her fingers. "Real good friends. Whatever she done, I done. I think she kind of used that on Maggie and Don. Don didn't actually want her. Then suddenly, Amy got pregnant. I didn't know at first. I knew things were strained between her and Don. When she told me about this, she cried because Don didn't want the baby. A bit later—I don't know how long, but it wasn't long, maybe a few weeks or a month—she said to me as we walked down the stairs from the flat, 'Will you be my bridesmaid?' I laughed. 'Who are you getting married to?' I said. 'Don,' she said. Well, I almost fell downstairs."

"Why was it such a shock?"

"Amy had given birth to a daughter, Joan. And Joan wasn't Don's child but his sister."

"How do you know this?"

"One night, when I was going for a bath, I had to pass the kitchen, where Gran and your mom often had their secret talks. The door was slightly open, and I heard Gran say that Amy had had the baby on February the fifteenth or some such day and then a lot of heavy whispering. *So she had the baby*, I thought. *It doesn't bother me*. But a few days later, when I saw the baby for the first time, it dawned on me that Don couldn't possibly have been the father. Like Granpa, he was a bricklayer; he had served his time as an apprentice with Granpa. He often went to England with him because the work was seasonal, and they could make a lot more there than here. Don sometimes went with Granpa, sometimes alone. He had been away by himself for all the summer months the year before. Granpa was at home the whole time."

"So Uncle Don couldn't have been the father," I said to clarify this for myself. "Did my mom know about this?"

"She knew."

"And Don?" I asked. "He and Granpa were always so close."

"Dad was a prick there too."

It was the first time I'd ever heard Betty being critical, even contemptuous, especially where her father was concerned. This family tale was spinning into larger and larger circles that never seemed to complete themselves.

"What in particular were you thinking of?"

"One day, after I knew about this, Don came into the kitchen as I was making my tea. He was reaching into the cupboard for some bread, and I asked him, 'Are you and Amy getting married?' Don slammed the loaf of bread down on the counter and replied, "Aye, and what're you goin' to do about it?' I wasn't trying to push anyone's buttons but just wanted to understand what was goin' on. 'Nothin',' I said, and walked out the kitchen. That's all that was ever said about it in my presence. Don never even spoke to Granpa about it. We were all so naive then. It didn't take me down in any way. It didn't take me up. I just accepted it."

Betty's acceptance of things was beginning to sound like my brother's shield, though understandably so.

"Robert told me about the mystery of the half cup of tea," I said, "and I'm wondering if you knew anything about this business. He and Gran came home one day to discover half a cup of tea left sitting on the table when no one was supposed to be home."

"Maybe it had something to do with what happened here—I don't know." Betty became thoughtful. "What I remember is that one day, Amy and me had arranged to go out some place for one o'clock. We were sitting in the living room, and I said, 'C'mon, you better get ready.' 'I'm not going,' she told me. 'Why not?' I asked. Then my dad, who had been sitting in the other easy chair, reading the newspaper, said a bit coldly, 'She's not goin'.' My dad never spoke to me like that. Him and me were close. I went off to get ready, and then I left. I had gone down a couple of flights of stairs and realized I had forgotten something. I had to knock to get back in, because I had no key. Dad opened the door. He had no shoes on.

"You never answered the door in those days without your shoes on, especially him. He was so careful about how he dressed when he wasn't at work. I walked past him and got what I'd forgotten. Amy was nowhere in sight, but on my way back out, I could see into Granny and Granpa's room because the door was partly open. I saw Amy's nylon stockings hanging over the chair. I remember thinking as I walked back down the stairs, *What if Granny came in? Somethin's goin' on there.* I forgot all about this until the baby came along. Then it all seemed to click together."

"Did you say anything to anyone about this?"

"No, I don't recall that I did. Don didn't say anything about the baby at the time. He just accepted it. So why shouldn't I? This is how we thought then. Why were we so naive?"

"What about Gran in all of this?" I asked.

"I just don't know why she went on accepting these things. She was very religious—I know that. But I can't answer that question."

"How did Mom deal with it?"

"Your mom was like Gran, very religious, in the early days. A Girl Guide who used to go to church. But somewhere along the line, she fell in love with dancin', started smokin' and drinkin'."

"Like father, like daughter?"

"Maybe it was his tomfoolery that changed her, but she never got like him. And she never accepted Amy. She and Gran were always getting onto Don about her—even after they were married. I could hear the four of them arguin' in the kitchen. Maggie and Gran thought that Amy had tricked Don into taking her baby as his own. I think that's what the argument was about one morning when Amy had a glass milk bottle in her hand. In the heat of the argument, hot-tempered Amy smashed it across your mom's face. I don't know whether it left a mark on your mom, but she had cuts all over her face then. Your mom was lucky not to lose her eye."

"Did Don never say anything to you about it?"

"Not until he came to visit me in Canada a few years ago. He said to me, 'Joan's not my daughter; she's my sister.' I was shocked—not because I didn't know, but because this was the first time Don had ever said anything to me. 'Don,' I said, 'I've known that for forty years. Maggie forewarned you. So did I, really.' What was he thinking of all those years? I guess by this time, he felt he could speak of it, since he was now divorced from Amy."

Betty had another coughing fit. Each one seemed worse than the others. I suggested we take a break and carry on later. Eileen came in to offer us some tea and cakes. The party was still going on. I went off to join the others. Betty went to bed. I had worn her out, though she was loath to admit it.

17
The Thread Finally Broken

The telephone calls from the hospital are becoming more frequent. Now it seems someone is calling every other day. This morning, the call comes at around eight thirty, just as I finish breakfast. It's another doctor, one I don't recognize and whose name now escapes me. I am already on guard.

"Mr. Glascoe, the night staff was trying to reach you earlier this morning. They left messages for you."

"They did?"

"Yes. You didn't get them?"

"No, I didn't." I hadn't heard the phone ringing and hadn't yet picked up the messages on my answering machine.

"I'm very sorry. I don't know what happened. In any event, I guess this is the first time you're hearing this."

"Hearing what?"

"Mr. Glascoe, I'm afraid your mother passed away this morning at around three o'clock."

Passed away, he says. Gone. Forever. Dead. My mother's dead. I try to comprehend. But it's useless. Her death is just there like an impenetrable black wall.

"I know it's not the best time to talk about this, but have you made funeral arrangements? Or would you like us to take care of that for you?"

"I've taken care of it, thanks."

"In that case, would you ask the funeral director to contact us?"

"Of course."

"Would you like to see your mom before she goes?"

Before she goes? I think. *Where is she going?*

"On the last and endless journey to nowhere," the voice of my madman whispers.

"Yes, I would."

"Just come up to the nursing station, and one of the staff will take you down to the mortuary."

The mortuary. Already?

"They don't waste any time," the madman's voice whispers again. "She's packed up and prepared for shipping."

"I'll be there shortly," I tell the doctor, and I hang up.

I don't cry. I just sit there staring into space. There are no tears, just a great emptiness. I wander from room to room. Then I try to do something, such as cleaning up the kitchen, until I realize I am disoriented. I sit down again and try to focus on the practical. There are relatives to be notified—Adèle, who's attending to her own ailing father in Guyana; Robert and his family; Ana; Uncle Don; and Aunt Betty. That's it. No one else. There's not a single friend left who might wish to know.

The reactions are predictable. Robert is shocked. He hasn't been prepared for this. I realize now that I should have let him know sooner about how serious her condition was. But I had seen her this way before, and she had come through. To avoid being melodramatic, I ended up cheating my brother of a last chance to see his mother alive.

I can't reach Aunt Betty in Saskatchewan or Uncle Don in Scotland until later in the day, and I have to leave a message for Ana at work to call me back. When she does, she takes it calmly.

"Are you okay, Dad?" she asks.

"Yes. I'm fine."

"I'm going to cancel my weekend trip."

"No, Ana, don't do that."

"Why not?"

"The living are more important than the dead. Take care of yourself. Nothing's going to happen over the weekend."

"That's why I don't want to go. I want to help you."

"Fine," I say with some relief. "If you would like to stay, I would be glad of the company and the help."

"Are you sure you're all right?"

"Yeah, I'm all right. I just have to avoid feeling sorry for myself. Your nana's better off now."

"She's free from all that pain."

"Precisely."

"Do you want me to come home from work?"

"No. I have to run over to the hospital. Do you want to see her?"

"No … I don't think I can handle that."

I get off the elevator at the eighth floor for the last time and run into Connie as she is helping someone move a trolley. She holds out her hand and offers her condolences.

"Just give me a few minutes," she says.

I wander into my mother's room. Her bed and pillows are stripped bare; the curtain on the window is drawn. The Kangaroo feeder is gone. All evidence of her presence has been removed.

Mrs. Garceau is in bed, lying on her back, snoring. Mrs. Henry is sitting up with her eyes and mouth wide open, as if she's just had a shock. Adrienne is by her side, eating a curry breakfast from a plastic container she has brought from home. For the first time since I have met her, there is no smile on her face. She stops eating, stands up, and, with a little embarrassment from just swallowing her sweet potato, reaches out toward me. We hold hands like old friends.

"How are you?" she asks with genuine concern.

"I'm fine. My mother's better off, really."

"She's at peace now. You were so good to her, you know. So loyal."

I start to feel sorry for myself. Tears well up in my eyes.

"It's been a pleasure knowing you," I say in an effort to cut this line of conversation off.

"You look okay, you know," she says, attempting to reassure me.

"Good-bye, and all the best," I say, awkwardly leaving the room.

I wander up and down the hallway while I wait for Connie to take me to the mortuary. They're all there, my fellow wanderers: the man in the diaper, head bowed, muttering to himself as he dawdles from room to room; Ali, eating a banana while he lumbers through the halls on his endless search for a cigarette; the white-haired Victor, pulling himself along, hand over hand, on the handrail attached to the wall, as if he's measuring its entire length for a purpose known only to himself; the Chinese man, as usual, tailing the medication nurse; and the wheelchair team lined up against the wall in various frozen postures, all semi-consciously watching the traffic to and from the elevators, among them the sad, lonely lady in a flowery frock who says, "Good morning. How are you today?" as I pass and keep on going. I quietly take my leave of all of them.

I follow Connie to the mortuary downstairs. It's just an ordinary room except that it leads to another that is, in effect, a large refrigerator. A security guard unlocks a big padlock on giant wooden doors that have steel hinges. Then, without looking at us, he leaves. *This is where they keep the dead,* I think to myself, *to prevent them from rising up against the living.*

Two large trolleys wait inside, one empty and the other carrying a crumpled white plastic bag. Connie steps inside and wheels this one out before I begin to realize that the apparently empty bag contains the surprisingly thin, bony body of my mother. Connie dutifully unzips the bag. I ask her to leave me alone for a few minutes. I want to take this in.

I touch the crown of her head in a feeble Buddhist gesture and whisper, "Good-bye, my darling, good-bye." Her face is stone cold, her open mouth twisted, and her tongue sticking out, frozen forever in the gesture of the child she had become. I had worried that this moment might be difficult, but it isn't. My mother's forehead, incredibly, shows no signs of the agonizing struggle she has endured for so many years. The constant pain and stress around the eyes are gone. She looks more rested than I've ever seen her. She's been released from all the suffering. Adrienne's cliché is ironically apt. She's clearly at peace.

Her body is stripped bare, no less dignified for that. This is how she died. Her arms are folded over her breasts. The skin on her belly is as smooth as a baby's. Her legs, which for so long were bent stiff and useless, now lie straight and strong. She still has the crotch of a girl—thick hair the same dark brown, remarkably, that I remember from the days when I was a little boy in her bathtub.

The stillness and the silence are now total, inside and out. The struggle is over. The thread is finally broken.

I go outside to the park. The sun shines. The leaves flutter gently in the wind. Birds sing. Children play.

This is how it is.

18
The Speedway

Growing up in early 1940s Britain meant being faced with challenges unlike those the British youth face now. Betty, Maggie, their two brothers, and their parents lived in a volatile time in one of Europe's poorest cities. Making a living, staying alive, was the task at hand for all, and everybody had to work together. All the able-bodied men had gone to fight the great battles, leaving the older and underage men and all the women to keep the country working in their absence. No one had much choice about what he or she could do in those years. You could go into the forces if they accepted you, work in the post office, or find a job in the factories. Bricklayers willing to travel, such as Granpa and Uncle Don, had the Blitz to thank for the work they got rebuilding London. Betty was a machinist, and my mother worked as a crane driver. I was going to say that they had no other options, but for women, these were dramatic new options opened up by the war, and ones that wouldn't have been there otherwise.

"I loved my job," Betty said with conviction, unaware of the irony I had observed earlier in my brother's case, that here she was speaking of the war years. "I loved my life on Saracen Street, too," she added quickly.

"Robert said exactly the same thing."

"There was a little window up above the door of our flat," she continued, "that let in the light from a skylight on the landing outside. So we had a bright, beautiful hallway. There were three big rooms, all different colors, with huge windows—the blue room, the pink room, and the black room, which wasn't really black, but that's what we called it after I fell asleep in there and locked everyone out. We all lived there very happily most of the time. Robert too. He loved living with us. Robert wasn't a spoiled little boy, but we all babied him a bit. Uncle Andrew and Uncle Don wouldn't lift a hand against him. I often took him out with me. Granny especially loved him, and even Granpa did too. Your mom treated Robert like a king. He was always well dressed for school in Glasgow. But after the war, things began to change. Eventually, when your dad came home, they all went back to Cleland and then to Newarthill. A few years later, Robert went to high school in Motherwell."

"Bellshill," I corrected her.

"What?"

"Bellshill—it was about halfway to Glasgow, which is why I think he chose to go there."

"Yes, well, he often came back to us on Saracen Street. In fact, he played hooky from school and came to stay there most of the time."

"I never quite knew what the story was. As a child, I felt his absence during those years. He just wasn't around."

"He ran away from home, and at first, your mom didn't know he was at Gran's. He lived in an unhappy household. It was his life in Newarthill—listening to all the arguing—that did it."

"He later ran away to Canada. Following you. Why did you come here?"

"I got married in '46. Your mom told me my friends weren't good enough for me. I wanted to ask Helen Burns to be my bridesmaid, but according to your mom, Helen 'didn't know nothin'!' Then I wanted Peggy McAvoy. But Peggy wasn't suitable either. So your mom chose my bridesmaids. I had a girl standing up for me I didn't even know. Her name was Mary Ferguson. She was a nice woman, but she was Maggie's friend, not mine."

"Is that why you left Scotland after you were married?"

"Well, I married a Canadian airman, and he wanted to go back to Canada. Seemed like a good idea to me. I guess I wanted to get away from all the fightin'."

"Sounds like both you and Robert ran away from home permanently and both to Canada."

"Yeah, Robert was like me in a way. He wanted to stay clear of all the trouble too. He had asked me about Canada when I was back for a visit in the '50s, and I encouraged him to come. I told him Pat and me would help him. I remember when he finally arrived at our place in Saskatchewan a few years later, I told him that I'd learned from your mom that your father was making plans to come to Toronto. You should've seen his face fall. He wasn't happy at all at that news. I guess when he left, it meant you were left there on your own after that. What was it like for you?"

"That was 1957. I remember it clearly. There was always a lot of fighting going on," I told her. "I would be in bed at night with the lights out, and I could hear them yelling and tossing things around. I don't know if there was much hitting. I never saw any bruises. But there was a lot of noise."

"I had been to see them," she said, "in Newarthill when I was back on my visit. Your mom was patting a kitten on her knee in the living room. Sure enough, she and your dad got into an argument. He grabbed the kitten by the scruff of the neck and threw it against the wall."

"Did he kill it?"

"It was badly injured, and it had to be put down. Your mom was broken-hearted."

"What was the argument about?"

"Nothin' I can remember. They argued about anything. Your mom was strong-headed, and your dad wasn't a sociable guy. I couldn't really understand what was happening between the two of them then—or anytime."

Every once in a while, because of her emphysema, Betty had a coughing fit that took an enormous amount of her energy to endure. But now she was as hooked on telling these stories as I was on hearing them, sharing such old memories with one who remembered some of them or had experienced the fallout. Our mutual remembrance seemed to breach the boundaries of time. Even the pauses in our conversation opened up new tracks of recollection. Betty's memories of the 1940s now began to flow into memories of the '60s and then the '80s and back and forth a few times among them. The decades intermingled easily in her mind.

When my parents came to Canada, Betty and Pat tried to lure them to the West. Bob and Maggie had lived almost all their married life in villages and small towns, and they would have mixed well with prairie people. They knew how to work hard for a living, and their lack of social graces would not have been so noticeable. My father, left to himself, would probably never have moved from the town of his birth, Cleland. The shift to Toronto was driven by my mother's obsession, an obsession with the idea of reuniting the family. Emigrating to Toronto was the sole passion of her life since her older son's arrival there after his brief stay with Betty in Saskatchewan.

"She wanted to be close to Robert," Betty said. "That was a big mistake."

"I couldn't agree with you more, but why do you say that?"

"She didn't get along with Elaine."

Neither my mom nor Elaine was easy to get along with. Mom was uncompromising about everything; Elaine was deeply insecure about her husband. Both women were possessive in the extreme, and each was as abrasive as the other. This was a bad mix.

"Elaine was jealous because your baby, Ana, was the first grandchild by a day—and a girl, to boot—while hers was second and a boy, Bobbie." Betty always cut to the bone. She had a way of simplifying things that made eminently good sense.

"What difference did it make?" she added with indignation. "Why start a fight over something like this? And why move to Toronto? I tried to talk them out of Toronto. There were no jobs there when they came."

"The old man," I recollected, "could only get security-guard jobs, and Mom worked as a waitress in a diner."

"I couldn't understand how she could leave Gran," Betty said, "them being so close for so long. So attached too. I remember one time, I wrote to Gran while Granpa was still alive and invited them here, all expenses paid. I got a letter from your mom telling me that Gran wasn't well enough to travel and that asking her to take a trip like that was disgraceful. I thought I'd done something wrong. After your mom arrived in Toronto, you'll remember that somehow Gran was able to come to Canada then. Your parents had very little money, but they somehow paid her fare to Toronto, never asked me for help.

"Gran sat there in that little apartment, never going anywhere. I wrote her directly and asked her if she'd like to come to the farm. We flew her up. She loved wandering around the yard with Gord, watching the turkeys getting fed, baking bread, and going with us to bingo. Then a letter came from your mom to say that if she wasn't home by your birthday, she needn't come at all. We had her for a month, and your mom had her for about six. Why couldn't it be half and half? She was just so possessive about Gran. Always."

I knew nothing of this letter, and I'd had nothing to do with getting Gran back on time for my birthday. It was just my mother's excuse to satisfy her greed for the heart and soul of Gran. It wasn't easy for me to accept, but Ana's words were echoing in my brain: "She kept her nasty side from you."

"When the two of them came to Stoughton years later," Betty continued, "long after they had emigrated to Canada, we drove them to Weyburn, where we owned a house. Your dad asked if we would rent the house to them. I told him yes, that was fine. He loved the garden. Maggie loved the house. I said, 'You're welcome to it.' So they stayed there for a few days to see how they liked it. I think they even phoned you to tell you they were going to take it."

"They did. And I was delighted. Their life in Toronto was miserable. I couldn't imagine a better scenario for them than living out on the prairies near you."

"When Pat and me went back to Weyburn to take them out to supper, everything had changed. Somethin' was wrong. She wasn't feeling well. She had decided she wasn't going out to supper. Pat talked her into it. I asked her if she wanted a drink in the restaurant before dinner. She said no. So I said, 'Well, I'll have a rye and Coke,' and Pat asked for a Tom Collins. Your dad said, 'I'll have the same.' That was that, but Maggie wouldn't order any supper.

"The next day, she said to me, 'We won't be takin' the house in Weyburn.' I was shocked. I asked her why. 'It seems I have to come all this way for Bob Glascoe to do something I've wanted him to do for years!' she cried in a huff. 'What was that?' I asked. 'When you ordered a drink, he ordered the same.' This was flabbergasting to me. 'I ordered rye and Coke, and he got a Tom Collins.' But I couldn't convince her that this was true. I asked Bob and Pat when they came in, and sure, I was right. But it made no difference to her. This is the reason she gave for not coming to Weyburn."

"I never understood that decision," I said. "I couldn't get an ounce of sense out of her at the time. What was she getting at? That there was something between you and Dad?"

Betty faltered on some of my more sensitive questions.

"Once she did. No, I think she wanted … I don't know what she was really getting at."

But Betty did know, and I knew she knew. But I had to prompt her a bit more. I wanted to know about that "once."

"You know, Betty, I don't have any illusions about my mom and dad. I've seen some very odd things in their lives, and I've done a few odd things myself. So don't worry about my sensitivities."

The question about my dad took us backward again, back to the cobbled streets of the old shipbuilding city that she once called home— back to Glasgow shortly before the war, not long after Mom and Dad were married.

"I was about seventeen. This chap I knew—that's how we politely referred to guys then—asked me one day at work if I would go to his house for the weekend. I wasn't a loose woman," she said, laughing herself into another fit of coughing. "But everybody lived with their families, and if we went to each other's homes, we were well chaperoned. He had a sister, and I was to sleep with her. I didn't even like this fellow, but he worked with Granpa and Don in Glasgow, and that's how I got to know him. Anyway, I went out to the pictures with him, as we called the movies over there, but in the end, I didn't go with him to his place."

I wasn't sure how this related to the story Betty was about to tell me, but I think it served as reassurance, if I needed it (which I didn't), that there were men in her life and that she had no interest in my father.

"When I got home later that night, Gran, as usual, was knitting away.

She looked a bit upset. I said, 'What's wrong?' She replied, 'Maggie and Bob.' 'What about them?' I said. She wouldn't say. I kept pestering her until she did. Maggie told her that she had been out shopping that day and when she came home, 'She found you and Bob kissing in the corner.'"

Betty's mouth opened wide as she shook her head in disbelief even now.

"'She *what!*' I said. 'I know, Betty—I know you wouldn't,' Gran said. 'I've been at work all day, for God's sake!' I insisted. I thought for a minute that Gran didn't believe me. 'I believe you, Betty. I believe you,' she claimed. Gran decided she was going the next day to Cleland, where your folks were living, to get to the bottom of this. 'I'll go with you,' I said. 'No, no,' Gran said, 'you might just make things worse.' This is a bad thing to say to someone who's innocent. How can you make things worse if what you're supposed to have done isn't true? Anyway, Gran went to see them.

"Now, in those days, your mom always held the pay packets. Your dad got pocket money and cigarettes. But now because of this thing that supposedly happened with me, she wasn't giving him anything—no money, no cigarettes. Gran went back and forth every few days during this period, and nothing had changed. After her fourth visit, I asked her, 'Did Bob get a cigarette yet?' 'Aye,' Gran said, 'he got one.' So I asked, 'How come?' 'He admitted it,' she said with her head bowed.

"Your dad admitted that he was kissing me just to get a cigarette. This caused me a lot of pain. But I always thought that Gran believed me until a long time after this, when I was back in Scotland in the '60s on another visit from Canada. I was lying in bed, with Gran close to sleep as she blathered away—you know how she was—talking about the latest big fight your mom and dad had. He was supposed to be running around with his brother's wife, Molly. Was that true, by the way?"

"I don't know. I never saw any hard evidence, and Johnny Glascoe, in all the time I knew him, didn't even drop anything close to a hint that any such thing had ever happened."

"You and your mom saw your dad sitting on a bus or something."

"Yeah, Mom said he was coming from Molly's. But I could never confirm that."

"Right. Maggie just jumped to conclusions. Now, where was I?"

"In Scotland with Gran in the 1960s."

"Oh, yes, Gran told me all about this and said to me, 'Just look what he tried to do with you, Betty, when you were a young girl.' I was half asleep, but when she said that, I woke up with a start and jumped out of bed. 'What's wrong?' Gran asked. 'For years, you always told me you believed me,' I said to her, 'and now here you are more or less accusing me all over again.' I never forgot that, and I felt really hurt that my mother had really never believed my story. In fact, I never quite got over it. I had all the proof anybody needed: I was at work the whole time! Your dad never, ever laid a finger on me."

I didn't do much of a job defending my dad, because I had been taken in by these stories too. I was still having trouble adjusting to the new truths about Mom. She had done a masterly job of controlling how I saw my dad, and he was not the kind of man who knew how to defend himself on this score.

"Anyway, it was because of this that I never believed the story about your dad and Molly," Betty asserted. "I kept thinking back to that nonsense about me an' him after the war. Your dad had been forced to admit that something happened that never did."

It was time for another coughing break. I went off to Eileen's kitchen to get Betty a glass of water. Betty had become more diminutive in later years, and her chest was concave from poor health. So when she heaved to cough in these almost-convulsive fits, it was as if she were going to burst the thin skin and shatter the skimpy bones of her upper body. It was a distraction for both of us, though, and released the tension in the story by shifting the conversation to something else. She never flinched in her commitment to carry on with the story. So when she was ready to start again, I went back to something she had raised earlier.

"What else did you know about the affair Mom had with Rankin during the war?"

"To tell you the truth, it didn't interest me at all, and I never took much notice of it. More unusual things had happened in our house, so there wasn't much in this that could shock me. They used to go to the pictures together, and he sometimes came to the house, though I never

157

actually saw him there. He didn't want to face me, you see, because I worked for him at Mains'. Gran wasn't happy with the situation, but she never said anything to your mom about it that I heard.

"Rankin was no ordinary guy. He was a big shot at Mains', a manager who could hire you or fire you. He was hooked on your mom. She was a beautiful girl, and she knew it. Even in the factory—where, like the rest of us, she wore a headscarf tied up in a turban knotted at the front, overalls, and work boots—she turned the men's eyes. She was picked once to present a trophy to the winner of the speedway rider's championship at Hawthorn Park."

The speedway was thrilling. It consisted of four motorcyclists at a time, racing around a shale or gravel track at high speeds, one foot down to steady themselves around the two curves. The smell of the burning rubber and spent fuel and the dust rising in clouds from the track heightened the excitement. The riders lined up behind a tape much like horse riders at the derby, leaned forward over their wide-angled handlebars, and revved their engines so high that you thought your ears and your heart were going to burst.

The start in such a condensed track was critical, and the riders had a peculiar way of doing the bends on the slippery gravel. They would lift their butts off the seats, drop the bikes down as low as possible, turn the front wheel up and forward for steering, and broadside, or slide the bike around the turns sideways. The gravel would spray up violently against the wire netting, which really didn't provide much protection to those of us who wanted to get right down on the track. Winning depended on exceptional skill in managing the bends more than anything else. The small scale of this sport, the tightly packed huddle of the four riders, the condensed nature of the track, and the brevity of the races (four times around) made it intense and electrifying.

"It was Ashfield Park in the days I knew it," I told her. "I think she presented the trophy to somebody called Kenly Britain?"

"Yeah, that's right."

It occurred to me that my mother had always been on a speedway, turning, turning, turning in a cycle of sorrow and joy. She was the rider who never won the trophy, because she was always too busy looking to the left and the right, worrying about who was coming up behind her. In her distraction, she didn't notice that they were already far ahead, and in the end, she lost her bearings and never finished the race.

Betty's coughing was not the kind that improved. It only seemed to get worse the longer she sat up. I was always wary of continuing beyond some undefined threshold of tolerance, but she made no sign of letting up or wanting to let up. I went off, however, to make some tea and give her a rest.

19

Silence like a Shadow

I can't help noticing that my brother is beginning to stoop. He does not enunciate his words clearly. At this point, I don't know why. "Will the casket be open for me to see her now?" he asks as we step into the funeral parlor.

"I don't know," I reply since I've arranged to have it closed for the visiting hours.

We are dressed in suits for this occasion, which is not much of an occasion after all. We agreed that we would have no ceremony or service at the funeral home since no one outside of a handful of family members would be there. The funeral home is like any other: a combination of chintz overload and hyper-friendly stuffed shirts.

Cameron and an unfamiliar attendant, both of them like used-car salesmen, are waiting by the door to greet us.

"Hi, Mr. Glascoe," says Cameron. "I've opened up the casket for your brother to view your mother, and I have the papers ready for you to sign."

I introduce Robert before we are shown into the room of Mrs. M. Glascoe. It's a long, spacious room with a grey flower-covered coffin set up like an altar at the other end. Cameron is skilled at his job and knows when to make himself scarce. Robert approaches the casket with some hesitation. I follow behind. He puts his hand on the side of the grey box and nods as if he were checking to make sure it's her. We are looking at our mother for the last time. The mouth is now firmly closed, and her lips are stretched unnaturally across her face. But she looks years younger and more like the woman I knew, the one who had an identity and a personality.

I leave Robert alone to say his good-byes. I must tally up the costs, sign the papers, and close the deal. Dying isn't free.

Later, only six people gather in the room to pay their respects. Besides my brother and me, Adèle, Ana, and, unexpectedly, Maria and her sister, Jill, are here. The absence of my brother's family is palpable. We stand in a circle, cowed by the presence of death in the closed casket beside us and the emptiness of the large room. Soundlessness hangs like a shadow around us.

"It's hard to know what to say," I croak in an effort to break the ice. "Maybe we should have a rousing party."

"Like the Irish," Robert adds, "who insist on getting drunk."

The conversation has begun. It revolves around work and places we live in. Eventually, we start to laugh. No one asks about my mother. I know they're wondering. So I tell them the story of her last few hours. This brings another hush to the conversation. Soon it's time to leave. I ask them to sign the visitor's book and come to my place for a drink. Everyone accepts, but not without the consciousness that we are leaving someone behind forever.

Sitting by the door, as if my mother had carefully placed it there herself before she climbed into the box, is her battered old suitcase containing the last of her personal effects. Inside are two sweaters, a couple of blouses, an unused T-shirt, a flowery summer skirt and top, a nightdress, underwear, a pair of white socks with her name tag, a hairbrush, a set of false teeth in a plastic box, a white silk rose from an old corsage, and a musty smell.

"All the worldly goods of one Margaret Glascoe," Robert comments sardonically. "One lousy suitcase."

As we ride back in the car, he weeps openly. I touch his shoulder in an ineffectual gesture. We say nothing. We come to a dead halt at the traffic light and stare straight ahead. There is nothing more to say.

We too, just like our mother and all the mothers before her, slip into the big silence that closes like the night around the earth. Perhaps it's not as horrifying as we make it out to be. In the end, a release from the need to utter sound is something of a solace from the chatterbox violence of this rough world.

I think all this, but I say nothing more to my weeping brother.

20

Beginnings and Endings

In the 1970s, I had hitchhiked across Canada with Ana, who was then only ten years old. One of the best times we had was the time we spent with Pat and Betty at their farm in Stoughton. Pat was a heavyset man with fine facial features and a deep understanding and sharp intelligence nurtured by a lifetime of working to eke out a living from the land. He was honest and generous, without thinking of himself in this way. One of his oddities was that he didn't own a credit card and used banks as little as he could. In fact, he looked as if he had just robbed one every time he pulled out the wad of twenty-dollar bills he carried in his pocket to pay for all his purchases.

Betty was born and raised in Glasgow and was well into her mid-twenties before she came to Canada after the war. When you saw her here, though, with Pat on their farm, she seemed to have grown out of the landscape. There was a natural, unpretentious quality about her, a freedom from ostentation of any kind. There were no bells and whistles in her appearance or in what she said. As with Pat, the idea of standing on ceremony never occurred to her. I was reminded of all this now as I listened to the final part of Betty's story of my mother's last visit to their farm.

"The last time your mom came to Stoughton was after your dad died. She brought the cat with her."

Circe was a chorus that was repeating itself many times in this story. It was a study in itself, the object of Mom's obsessive attachment when my father was no longer around to assume that role. Circe was a house cat, meaning that she never once ventured outside of the one-bedroom apartments my parents lived in. I have to take responsibility for giving Mom the cat as a kitten. I'd rescued it from a careless owner, not realizing that the poor beast was going to be subjected to my mother's madness. At the time, she and Dad lived in the Lido, which had a rule against animals in the building, so Mom never even let the cat up on the windowsill, in case the neighbors saw it. She would tie Circe up on a leash when she was out.

After Dad died, Mom became paranoid, afraid of everything that moved, and had a penchant for keeping the house locked up like Fort Knox. The cat had no other model for its behavior. Even when I, a regular visitor, came to see her, Circe would take off under a chair and lie there hissing and growling at me. It was inconsolable. If ever a creature needed an animal psychologist, it was Circe. I can't imagine how such an animal behaved on the farm during the visit to Stoughton.

Betty continued her reminiscing. "Your mom asked me if I'd sleep with her, and I said I would. I didn't mean I wanted to sleep in a room in steamy July weather with all the windows closed and a cat lying beside us. I got up after I thought she'd fallen asleep, and she said, 'Where are you goin'?' I said, 'The bathroom,' because of course I couldn't tell her what I was up to. When I got back, I tried to open the window, but she'd have none of it. 'The cat'll get out,' she cried."

Circe became the one constant in Mom's life. Mom was pathologically afraid of losing the cat, though the beast would have been better off lost. This wasn't the only thing Mom was afraid of after my father's death, according to Betty.

"I didn't often argue with her, because she didn't seem to listen," she said. "But once, when we were in the kitchen, we got into a bit of a fight. She asked me if she could call you. I said, 'Yes, of course, but don't cry.' Every time she'd call you, she'd weep and cry, and I didn't want you to think we were torturing her down here. This time, she phoned, and she was laughing away. So I was happy. I was making carrot soup in a big pot which was boiling on the stove. While your mom was still chatting on the phone, I suddenly remembered the soup and jumped up to turn down the stove. Next thing I knew, she was off the phone and strode across the room to stand stock in front of me with her face right in mine. 'You don't want me to phone my son,' she hissed like that cat. 'My son means the world to me!' And then she burst into a fit of cursing and swearing, using words I'd never heard coming out of anyone's mouth before. I couldn't understand what was happening. I think that when I jumped up, she thought I was mad because she'd been on the phone too long. I think it was then that I began to realize what Alzheimer's really meant."

"There was no reasoning with her then," I said. "I was very grateful to you when, after Dad's funeral, you talked to me about her coming out here. I remember warning you, though, that she was very ill and that this illness was very deceptive. You could talk to her on the phone at this point and not notice any problems. Only when you spent a couple of days with her could you get a sense of how overwhelming she could be."

"I had a horrible time. I remember you saying before we left Toronto, 'Make sure she eats.'"

"Yes, because when she was on her own, she ate almost nothing."

"She ate like a horse up here, whereas I didn't. I was so upset the whole time she was here."

"I know what you were going through," I said apologetically. "This is what my father had to endure just before his death, and it's what I had to face afterwards. I was seeing the signs. She would say and do peculiar things. These things were difficult for me to interpret at the beginning, however, because I had always known her to be peculiar anyway. Besides, it was kind of hidden in the caustic banter between her and my dad. He knew something was wrong, but he didn't know what it was, and he said nothing to me about it. Until the very end."

"She'd put something in her purse to keep it safe," Betty recounted. "She'd even tell me she was putting it there. Then, five minutes later, she'd be looking for whatever she had just put in her purse, except she wouldn't remember putting it there."

"She had a veritable fixation," I said, "on that purse. She would carry it everywhere she went, squeezed under her arm as if someone were about to snatch it from her."

"I thought back to the Weyburn incident, when she was here with your dad, and I wonder if the Alzheimer's had already set in by then, at such an early age. That was in '81, when she had just turned sixty."

"I think it, or something else, was developing even before that, when I was still in university in the '60s. Dad complained about her washing his sweaters in the washer and then throwing them into the dryer. They came out like baby sweaters, and we all laughed about it—until she did it about four or five times. I once said to her, 'Why did you do that? You know it shrinks them, and he can't wear them again.' She said, 'I forgot.'"

"I wonder if it was even there in childhood when she was growing up. There were a lot of things she'd say and do and then deny them. It makes you wonder. I don't know."

Was there any connection between my grandfather's crazy behavior and my mom's later peculiarities, or between her embarrassing oddities and the onset of Alzheimer's? Perhaps. Who knows? Was each one of us just turning in our own circle of time, reflecting or repeating the same things as all the others before us, but completely oblivious to this fact?

"Another thing on her last visit to our place," Betty continued, "was that she couldn't keep money in her pocket. I gave her money. Gord gave her money. Pat gave her money. We all gave her money, and yet she never seemed to have any. I don't know what she did with it all of it, but it was gone by the time she left."

"She either hid it somewhere never to be found again," I added, "or she bought the same things over and over."

"Yeah, when she was leaving, I told her to take the five jars of Coffee-mate on the shelf with her. She bought them, but we never used the stuff. She told me, 'I don't want it; I bought it for you.' I didn't want it either. I just gave it away."

This seems like a rather unfitting ending, but this is what my mother's life had been reduced to. Betty made a heroic effort to help her sister through the grief of my father's death, but now the full-blown Alzheimer's wore down the loyal sister who had seen my mother through so many other crises.

Betty started to cough again—the deep, chesty cough I'd heard on so many occasions by now, each time wondering how she could survive it. I was grateful to my aunt for taking me back almost to the beginning of the long story of my mother, at least the beginning we mistakenly tend to call it—the beginning that isn't really a beginning at all but the end of something else that none of us knows anything about. The beginning that is an ending that begins again. She had helped me to understand this in the case of my mother and her family.

As Adèle and I left early the next morning to drive to the airport in Regina, neither Betty nor Pat was up. We passed their bedroom with suitcases in hand. The door was ajar. They were lying side by side, Pat peacefully asleep on his back and Betty half on her side, her face flushed and strained from coughing in her sleep. Next to her lay a mask hooked up to two oxygen tanks that stood by the bedside.

I mouthed a last silent good-bye and hurried to the door.

21

Nobody Knew She Was There

Cemeteries are places I've always had a fondness for—not because I've any interest in being buried in one but because they are a refuge from the noise of the living and a curiously revealing record of their comings and goings, a place where we can reflect on our fear and denial of the dead.

It has been too painful for me to visit the gravesite of my parents in Birchmount Cemetery since my mother's death a bit over a month ago, but today I feel the odd need to see that they've arrived safely in their place of rest. Both of them were cremated, and neither I nor my family wanted a ceremonial burial, so we left all that to the undertakers. The marble tablets that mark the sites of the ashes are small and hard to find. I'm having trouble locating the name of Glascoe in the designated place. Eventually, I find my father's name and dates but not my mother's.

"Where's my mother?" I mischievously ask the receptionist back at the cemetery office, which is itself like a stately mausoleum.

"Excuse me?" she says quizzically. She's not used to jokes about the dead. Laughing is strictly forbidden.

"I can't find my mother's gravesite. It's supposed to be in section nine."

"Just a minute, sir, and I'll look for it on the map."

As she scans a large map book, other visitors are lining up behind me.

"What did you say her name was?"

"Margaret Glascoe. She's supposed to be next to my father, Robert Glascoe."

"Yes, here's your father, Robert, in section nine." She flips the pages of the big map book back and forth. "I can't see anything here about your mother."

I'm getting uncomfortable about this and look around. I don't want to get into an argument in front of an audience over the whereabouts of my dead mother, though the conversation is fast becoming something apparently scripted for the stage. She picks up the phone and calls her supervisor.

"I have a gentleman here looking for a Mrs. Glascoe, but I can't find her name on the map."

The supervisor appears and ushers me to his office.

"I understand you're looking for you mother, Mrs. Glascoe?"

"Yes," I say, trying to contain my burgeoning sense of the absurd.

"Your father is here for sure, and I know you have been to section nine to see him. But we have no record of your mother."

"How can that be? She was buried here over a month ago."

"I know this must be very upsetting for you, sir, but if she had been buried here, we would have a record of it. There is no record. The receptionist checked the map, and I checked our files twice. Your mother's ashes aren't here."

I suppose I should be upset and shocked at the indignity of all this, but I'm not. Actually, I'm making an effort to suppress a kind of hysterical laughter. I suddenly see myself in a Monty Python skit. I have an image of Michael Palin and Eric Idle dressed in kilts, maniacally digging up the graveyard to find the ashes.

"She's not on the map and not in the files. Gone missing, it seems," I say, biting my lower lip to prevent myself from grinning uncontrollably. I have to struggle to be serious. "Who then," I continue, "is going to take responsibility for this?"

"I'm sure there's an explanation for what's happened here, sir, but we manage the cemetery. We aren't in charge of the burials. Your undertaker is."

Bureaucracy, it appears, is bigger than death. Back at my apartment, I reflect on the irony that I'm still looking for my mother even after she's dead. I call the undertaker to ask for an explanation.

"Who was your attendant at the funeral?" the voice on the other end of the phone asks.

"Cameron," I reply, fortunately remembering his name because he was so good at playing his part in that earlier production.

"Unfortunately, I can't get him for you. He's no longer with us."

Under the circumstances, I wonder what that means. All of these conversations are turning into a zany kind of black humor.

"I can assure you, sir," the voice continues, "we'll get to the bottom of this. I'm going to investigate immediately, and I'll get back to you today."

A couple hours later, I receive a call. It's the president of the funeral home. This is clearly an important matter—a fact I've already begun to ponder.

"Mr. Glascoe, I am extremely sorry for the distress all this has caused. I'm pleased to say that we have found the ashes of Mrs. Glascoe."

"Where?"

"They were still in an urn at the crematorium."

"How do you know they were my mother's?"

"They were marked 'Mrs. M. Glascoe, 1920–1997.'"

What else could he say? If he couldn't find somebody's—anybody's?—ashes, there would be a large price to pay—literally, since I would have every right to sue. I'm in no mood, however, to pursue this line of thought or action. I'm thinking about a little ditty by the great Scottish songwriter Ewan McColl: "Nobody Knew She Was There."

> She walks in the cold dark hour before the morning
> The hour when wounded night begins to bleed
> Stands at the back of the patient queue
> The silent almost sweeping queue
> Seein' no-one and not being seen
> He who lies besides her does not see her
> Nor does the child who once lay at her breast
> The shroud of self-denial covers
> Eager girl and tender lover
> Only the faded servant now is left
> How could it be that no-one saw her drowning

How did we come to be so unaware
At what point did she cease to be her
When did we cease to look and see her
How is it no-one knew she was there

"This is inexcusable," says the voice on the other end of the phone. "I would vigorously discipline the person responsible—except he no longer works here. Happily."

"What next?"

"You have nothing to worry about. I'll take charge of the burial arrangements myself, and everything will be taken care of. Would you like to have a graveside ceremony? We'll send a limousine for you and your family."

Impressive—he knows the score on this little matter.

"No ceremony. I'll be relieved just to see my mother in her rightful place," I say.

The botched burial has made me acutely aware that my mother is just as elusive in death as she was in life. I smile at the thought that she never quite fit into the container that I or anybody else had tried to make for her and that even now, she seems to have escaped from the one she was to be buried in. I find myself chuckling as I imagine that her death might have been not only a release from the suffering but also a liberation from all the boxes that life constructed for her, that she is fluttering somewhere in the secret interstices of space-time, exulting in having eluded us all in her winged existence.

It seems oddly fitting that I'll never be sure where she is or who she was. It makes no sense to speak of her death as a closure. On the contrary, it's an endless opening.

22

Spiral of Blood

Igrieved my mother long before she died. On the day of her death, June 6, 1997, the grief was transformed into a compelling and fitful urge to embark on a hunt, as if searching for a kidnapped child, to find out what was happening in the world on the day of her birth, April 26, seventy-seven years ago. I didn't know then what the compulsion was, but in my urgency, I hurried to the library to look up the *Times* of London to read of the great and momentous events of the day. They were indeed duly reported to the British people by the *Times*, which, operating from something like a pre-Galilean mindset, considered the human race, at least in its Anglicized species, to be the center of the universe. Thus, the end of the so-called *Great* War was followed by a concern with *Great* War stories of the *great* enterprises of *Great* Britain, stories about the accomplishments of the *great* men and women who were charged with the responsibility—or saddled with the burden, depending on how you looked at it—of running the *great* nation.

There were stories about such people as Lloyd George, the Liberal prime minister who had succeeded in resolving a disagreement with the French over reparations to be paid to the Allies by Germany. This was important because it would lead to the issuance of a manifesto declaring the satisfaction of the conditions of the postwar peace treaty—a magnificent achievement, no doubt, especially since it meant that Germany would be disarmed and forced to pay "all that it is possible for her to pay and to become prosperous enough to pay more at the earliest practicable dates" as punishment for its aggression. It was also magnificent because it released the British government to deal with other pressing political matters like the so-called Irish situation, which was becoming increasingly tense, and economic matters, such as the speculation on the Italian lira, which was nearly out of control.

The writers and readers of this history cannot be faulted for not anticipating that in spite of these efforts, or perhaps because of them, the rise of fascism in Germany and Italy, civil war in Northern Ireland, and a worldwide depression would eventually come to pass. No, the *Times* and its readers were far too deeply immersed in the great matters of the present to be concerned about the future. "Red Russia," after all, was in the throes of a revolution in which "British subjects" in that country were being classified as bourgeois and treated—or, more to the point, *mis*treated—accordingly. Cultured and refined ladies were witness to the attacks suffered by fellow patriots and to the fact that Moscow was "one great cesspool of disease, corruption and iniquity." They were in a position to know that "the most refined girls of the upper and middle-classes were formed into companies and marched to clean the lavatories" in public places.

If history is not always concerned with such *great* events as these, it is concerned with momentous ones, events that are worthy of the attention of a people whose tradition and promise have destined them for greatness. This may be why the *Times* reported that a lieutenant of the Twelfth Battalion in the First Division of the Australian Imperial Force that defended the nation in the Great War "had the honor of being received by the King." And following this, His Majesty, "attended by the Gentlemen in Waiting, went to London" to hold counsel at Buckingham Palace, present at which were a right honorable secretary of state, a viscount, and a lord. The *Times* determined that there were other similarly stirring events, such as the queen's morning drive from Windsor Castle; Princess Mary's "promise to be present at a display of drill and physical exercises by local boys and girls clubs, scouts, girl-guides, and cadets"; the Duke of Newcastle's "week-end visit to London"; and the Duchess of Marlborough's excursion to Paris, where she was "to remain for some time."

Certain other matters transpired on this historic day that, though they pale in comparison, were important enough to deserve a mention in the *Times*, such as the urgent national "moral and physical need" for "open-air recreation"; Selfridge's new line of "faille silk handbags" that none could "afford to neglect" because they had the "inspired chic" necessary for the "tout ensemble" of the fashion-minded; or even just the weather forecast, which called for "fresh northwesterly winds, low cloud, local showers, with bright intervals and rather cold temperatures."

If the *Times* of London was concerned with nothing but the making of such history, it can hardly be blamed for that. If it barely squeezed into the corner of its pages the story of a former British officer who, though he had been decorated for his efforts in the Great War, was unemployed and had a family near starvation; the account of the eighteen-year-old girl who died from multiple stab wounds inflicted in broad daylight on the streets of London after a brutal attack by her destitute young lover; or even the report of widespread uprisings of the Mexican people against their government—if the *Times* barely mentioned such occurrences, it can surely be excused because a national newspaper cannot be expected to deal adequately with anything but matters that are of the utmost importance to the British people as a whole, or at least to those who consider themselves to be to be their representatives.

If the *Times* or any other chronicler of the British people had taken any notice of the birth of my mother, Margaret Telford McGregor, it would have told us only that she had no family ties or social connections to anything that could be considered important to the nation. She was just a Scottish working-class girl who, in the blustery town of Kincardine in the rolling, heather-covered countryside of Fife, struggled from her mother's belly moments before her brother. If the *Times* had followed her through life, it would have noted that though she showed a feistiness and tenacity from this day on, she achieved little that anyone beyond her immediate family would take notice of. She became a woman of no importance, a woman who never deserved to make it to the headlines of the newspapers or attained high office, accumulated any wealth, committed heroic acts, healed the sick, or changed the world.

She was just an ordinary woman most people weren't interested in.

She left school at sixteen after missing a train that would have taken her to university. She married a miner, gave birth to and raised two sons, "dutifully aided the war effort" as a crane driver in a munitions factory, emigrated to Canada, and ran a cafeteria in Toronto, all the while struggling and fighting with an alcoholic husband who eventually killed himself. If the *Times* had published her epitaph, it would have stated curtly that she battled Alzheimer's disease, eventually losing all her faculties in the process. She began in obscurity and ended in obscurity. This, in the estimation of the world that the *Times* reflects, was the sum total of her accomplishments—no more and no less.

I now understood why I was so driven to seek out the *Times*. Its very name blared out the irony of the way we pretend to construct our days, like counting blocks of vacuous chatter stacked in a column that teeters with every new block added to the spindly structure, forming the grand illusion of fossilized time we call history, the chatterbox history that we read about whenever we open the pages of a newspaper, thinking we have figured everything out—*Here it all is; this is the way things were.* Everybody says so with a hindsight that is another name for the blindness we all seem to succumb to.

I realized now that this great vehicle of collective human chatter helped me to resolve the lessons embedded in my mother's sad life—not because of what it said but because of what it didn't say, what it couldn't say: that her mute endurance of suffering was far too meaningful to be included as prattle in all the newspapers of the world. The lessons of this suffering came before all the words, before the clock and calendar, before we read the newspapers in the morning.

Bewildered by the dazzle of a world filtered through the multicoloured glass of the media, we think we're going forward into the future, evolving from the crude to the sophisticated, from the primitive to the developed. But the people and things who came before us are not so different from ourselves as we are now, each of us circling in an upward (or is it downward?) spiral, an endless helix of living and dying, loving and fighting, with its attendant joys and sorrows, pleasures and pains, happiness and suffering—a whirling vortex that all of us are unrelentingly drawn into. Revolving in the perpetual present that we never catch sight of, our lives circle into one another, always different in their sameness, always the same in their differences, each one a circle that never completes itself, a spiral that forever turns into others, all together turning, turning endlessly in the great, incomprehensible arc of time.

We audaciously speak of this as if we understand the marvellous confluence of matter and mind, guts and blood, bone and flesh, feces and urine, solids and secretions, thoughts and memories, hopes and dreams, sensations and emotions, moods and attitudes—presume to call this mesmerizing flux of energy "ourselves." *Ourselves*, we say, as if we owned it, as if we controlled it, as if we knew what it was all about, as if the word itself took hold of the reality, subjected it to our scrutiny, and made us the masters of our destiny. The strange syntax that is the mirror of language, however, only magnifies the mystery and reflects it back in reverse.

My mother's end had sent me back to her beginning, but I didn't feel as if I were going backward into the past. It was as though I were moving forward into the future. Actually, I was running to keep up with the present that always eluded my grasp, the days gone by opening up unrelentingly into those to come. In her past, I had discovered my future. Her life had spiralled out of her mother and father's and multiple others' before them that I knew nothing about, and it had spiralled into my brother's and mine, followed by mine into my daughter's, my daughter's into my grandchildren's, and theirs into those who are still to come, ones I will never know. My frantic search for my mother's identity had brought me face-to-face with the incredible mystery: that the past and the future dissolve into the unknown, the great unknown of the unknowable present that keeps on vanishing before our eyes. My mother's birthday and death day were neither the beginning nor the end of anything; they were simply the markers of the astonishingly rich enigma of time endlessly working itself out in the here and now that never arrives.

23

Dear Mother

This is the last letter I'll ever write to you and the only one you'll never receive.

The woman I thought I knew was the loving daughter unconditionally devoted to her mother; the overindulgent parent who doted on her own children and their children; the gutsy wife who, with feisty banter, struggled valiantly and loyally with a deeply depressed husband; the fighter with a backbone of steel who was ready to take on the world to protect and preserve her family; and a woman of uncommon intelligence hidden beneath layers of the usual banalities that make up the humdrum stuff of ordinary life.

What I have here in my hands—the testimony of your family, of all those who loved you most—tells a different story. When I read this now, I shake my head in wonder. Was it that they just didn't know you as well as I did, or is it I who didn't really know you? Each one of our family paints the picture of someone I hardly recognize. I want to know who you were, and I want the world to know the enormous struggle you endured and how you fared. Sure, you made mistakes, as we all do, but above all, I want everybody to forgive you.

Who were you really? You ought to know by now. Born Maggie McGregor, you married Bob, my father, and changed your name to Glascoe. To me, as a child, you were Mammy, which I subsequently shortened to Ma in my teens because the other sounded too childish. I now find myself referring to you as Mother. To Robert, you were always

Mum, which always seemed too polite in Scottish terms, or Mom, when he came to Canada. Your grandchildren called you Nana. Your husband mockingly called you other names when you began to do odd things. You were all these and many more. We all thought we called you by your true name. In the end, you didn't respond to any name at all. Now there's nothing left but names, empty names—names without a body, mind, or voice.

You loved us all in your own way, and you spilled a lot of blood doing it—your own blood and the blood of others. No, dear, I know you had no intention of doing violence to anyone. It's just that we all carry garbage inside us, and sometimes it gets the better of us. No one can live without creating it, and in your case, you faced enormous obstacles that would have destroyed many. Where did all the garbage come from? Living, darling—just living.

How strange the irony of your relationship with your husband, Bob, my poor, dear father. Your life together was a long-drawn-out battle for survival of the fittest. I know you were not just shocked but also traumatized by his death. I held you the day he died. Your hysteria was real and unmistakable. Taking his own life was a terrible kick in the guts. He had been there for you for such a long time—battling it out, to be sure, but each of you kept hanging on to the other just the same. Who knows why you stayed together all those years? Except that, in spite of all the misery you caused each other, love lingered on.

If you could have heard your sister, Betty, speak of your brilliance and beauty with such untrammeled admiration, you would never have been so jealous of her and so hurtful in your treatment of her. Do you remember how you accused her of kissing my dad? She vigorously denied it well after you and he were both gone. Didn't you realize how much you were loved here? No, dear one, I guess you didn't, and maybe that's why you mistrusted so many of those closest to you.

I know you'd be broken-hearted to learn that the son who left home so young—Robert, whose absence you never accepted, the son you pursued three thousand miles across the ocean—died a sad death from a brain tumour ten years after you. I wondered why he began to slur his words in midlife, almost as if he'd had a stroke. I never thought to mention it, because no one else seemed to notice. Incredibly, it seems as if the battalion of pins-and-needles specialists he consulted never performed an early brain scan. It would have been too late anyway. He died without ever getting over the deep scars left on his life from his childhood. I know you did your best, and you loved him dearly. He missed you as a boy, however, even when you were there. All that enormous love you had for him as a child wasn't enough to fill his empty heart. You were trying to raise him while still living your own young life and having to work six days a week, morning to night, in the only jobs around.

I'm your second son—yes, I always felt that way, second to Robert in your heart. I know, I know—you were proud of my educational achievements, which, to me, now are paltry in comparison with your accomplishments in life. What did you accomplish? An amazing capacity to endure amidst the most profound troubles. My suffering pales beside yours.

Remember the time you told us all you were leaving with the lodger? No, dear one, I don't blame you for that, especially now, looking back on all that happened, even though I never got over it. Hell, I didn't even know I wasn't over it until long after I got myself in trouble with the dearest women in my life. Oh yes, I travelled much the same road as you on that score, except that I've been married twice, the second time now for more than thirty years to dear Adèle, who has hung in all this time even though, like yours, this union has been a rollicking affair peppered by dalliances all too much like your own.

I'm so like you it's frightening. I look in the mirror, and your eyes are staring back at me. I cough when I'm sick, and I hear you. I walk with the same knobby bump you had on the same knee on the same leg. Where do I begin and you end? It seems so easy on the surface to distinguish us, but I know no more about myself than I do about you. Even now, after all the hunting and gathering I've done, it will seem to you that I'm still, at this late stage in my life, the child looking for his mother. It's true that I was looking for you in all my relationships, not because you were the model of contentment—does it need to be said?—but because I, like my brother before me, craved the love I never got enough of. No, darling, I don't hold you responsible for this. Just as you were caught in the spiral of suffering of those before you, I was caught in yours. Others have been caught in mine. Sadly, I've been unable to halt the flow of blood. So you see, I'm in no position to lay blame.

You would have been hurt to hear the testimony of your lovely granddaughter, Ana, but she told the truth, and you would have to face that. I like to think you would have been proud of her astonishing observational powers and the gift of caring that would have reminded you of Granny. She's now blessed in her second marriage with a loving and devoted husband, Tom, and they have two sweet children, Jack and Andrea. Jack is such a happy, cheerful, sensitive boy that I'm afraid you would smother him with your overwhelmingly robust attention. As for Andrea, she reminds me so much of you, the better you, the one with the remarkable promise all those years ago, before you refused to run to catch that train to the university—the scintillatingly intelligent, sharp-witted, feisty you that could hold her own with the very best. Andrea is so gritty and creatively mischievous. Nothing will keep her down, certainly not a missed train.

You might have been gratefully surprised, dear, to listen to young Bobbie, your other favourite grandchild, speak of you. He was so amazingly sensitive to your plight and unflagging in his resistance to his own mother's antipathy toward you, the champion who defended your good name. You'll be alarmed to hear, no doubt, that he has had his health troubles along the way, suffering from a rare kidney disease. But like dear old Granny, his get-up-and-go is remarkable. He too has been fortunate with his partner in life, Penny, and they have produced two wonderful kids, Stanley and Beverly. They are blessed with great gifts and promise that you helped to pass on through your eldest son.

Oh, I know you would be so proud of all your very own great-grandchildren.

I know too that you're probably not really worried about what your daughters-in-law said about you, but neither Maria nor Adèle expressed any bitterness. In fact, they were both amazingly gracious and conciliatory. They seemed, at some level, to understand the terrifying struggle you were going through, though I suspect you left wounds in Maria's heart that will never heal—wounds that I, of course, only made more painful. No, darling, Elaine had nothing to say. She probably feels the same way about you still as you felt about her—for understandable reasons, you must admit. There's no point in mincing words at this late stage.

Not to worry, however. I am here to tell you that I'm more than deeply grateful for some special things you did for me—too many, in fact, to list. Suffice it to say, you were my entry into this existence and, in the colossal silence of your departure, a doorway to its mystery. It was your sad and troubled life that precipitated the pondering that became the passion of my being, your agonizingly tragic death that taught me how to accept the exquisite futility of the search for answers. You gave me the chance to experience the enigma of our coming and going firsthand, to embrace the serene understanding that I don't need to understand, recognizing that it's all too big to merely understand. Even though you're a stranger to me still, I feel uncannily closer to you than ever before.

I nearly forgot something—the dancing. That's what I said: dancing. Yes, I know, you were *always* dancing, even when I was sleeping in your belly. I want to thank you for giving me my first and best lessons. You should see me now; I can do the quickstep and the fox trot, the waltz and the rumba, the hot-belly salsa, the merengue and the mambo. And my timing is impeccable, thanks to your wonderful teaching. You were my first dancing partner and the one who guides me now as I dance the night away.

Good-bye, Mammy darling, good-bye. I love you still.

24
The Whole of Her Happiness

Pausing in the shade
of an oak,
she studies
the shimmer of begonias,
reaches
for the delicate spray
of the sprinkler,
smiles
at the unbroken blue
of the sky,
exults
in the sensation of wind
on her cheek,
imitates
the impudent sounds
of a redwing,
laughs
uncontrollably at pigeons
jockeying for handouts.
This
is the whole of her happiness,
a moment
blissfully uncomplicated
by recollections of the past
or anticipation of the days ahead.